More than money...
More than faith ...

successfully raising missionary support in the 21st Century

· · · · · · · ·

Paul I. Johnson, Ph.D.

D1710741

Pleasant Word (a division of WinePress Publishing, PO Box 428, Enumclaw, WA 98022) functions only as book publisher. As such, the ultimate design, content, editorial accuracy, and views expressed or implied in this work are those of the author.

ISBN 13: 978-1-4141-0930-5
ISBN 10: 1-4141-0930-X
Library of Congress Catalog Card Number: 2006911221

Dedication

*This book is dedicated to you and all others
who seek to follow the Lord's command to go
into all the world and preach the Gospel
to everyone, making them His disciples.
May your work be faithfully supported by those
who have sent you and may the harvest
be fruitful and blessed by God.
Be faithful—God will do His part
and you will rejoice together with Him
when you see His harvest.*

Acknowledgements

There are several people to whom I am indebted as I worked through a lot of the issues mentioned in this book. Some offered a lot of encouragement and some were of great practical help.

Ray Posey encouraged me in the early days of my struggles and offered a sounding board for a lot of my thinking. His positive input and responses to my wonderings kept me on track. Marty Meyer kept after me to finish the book when at times I was ready to put it aside.

Shirley Swagerty edited and proofed the book and had a strong personal interest in seeing the book go to press.

Carolynn Andrews did the desktop publishing without charge. Being a former "faith" missionary, she had a vested interest in seeing that the point-of-view expressed in this book be made public. Carolynn also wrote the last chapter, "Creating An Attractive Newsletter," for which I am grateful.

Our partners, the individuals, families, and churches who have prayed for us, supported us financially, and who have encouraged us in other ways made the book possible. Without them, we would have dropped out of the missionary ministry many years ago.

Lastly, my wife Dona, who bore the struggles and challenges with me, deserves more credit than I can put into words.

Gratefully,
Paul I. Johnson

Table of Contents

The author has something to say, which he perceives to be true and useful, or helpfully beautiful. So far as he knows, noone has yet said it; so far as he knows, no one else can say it. He is bound to say it, clearly and melodiously if he may; clearly, at all events. In the sum of his life he finds this to be the thing, or group of things, manifest to him—this, the piece of true knowledge, or sight, which his share of sunshine and earth has permitted him to seize. He would fain set it down forever; engrave it on the rock, if he could; saying, "This is the best of me; ...this, if anything of mine, is worth your memory."

—Ruskin, *Sesame and Lillies*

A Bit of History

I've been working with missionaries in the domain of support raising for more than twenty years.

There are two men from different seminars that I taught whom I'll never forget.

Both were college students. Both considering ministries with mission organizations. That's why they signed up for the seminars. Well, that's why I thought they signed up.

One young man, even before I was finished with the introduction, brought me to a startled halt by jumping up, and saying loudly, "I will never be a beggar!" and walked out. He must have come just to make that statement. But he didn't give me the opportunity to tell how much I agreed.

The other young man, at a different time and place, stood up right in the middle of the seminar while I was discussing the issue of living by faith, and said, "I've been duped!" then turned around and walked out.

These men were expressing some deeply imbedded thoughts and feelings about raising support. Raising support can bring out some intense feelings, and sometimes passionate expressions of those feelings. Some people have said that the thought of raising support is what turned them off to missions.

It will never be known how many men and women are lost

to missions over the kinds of misunderstandings expressed by these two men, and shared by others, but I do know this kind of reaction is unnecessary. My hope is to present raising support in such a way that it cannot be used as a reason for rejecting the call of God on one's life.

Part of the reason for the fear of raising support is misunderstanding what it really means to live by faith. There is quite a lot of confusion about this ideology (as witnessed through the two young men mentioned above). That is why the beginning chapters of this book are about the historical development of, and Scriptural basis for, raising support.

There is confusion. There is confusion among the principals involved: churches, missionaries, and mission agencies.

One thing I would like to accomplish is to help bring missionaries, mission agencies, pastors, mission committees, and churches into closer harmony. The support-raising model presented in this book will make a significant contribution to this end. Wouldn't it be helpful if we could all agree on a model, a way of doing it?

I will not be getting into the profound discussions going on in some circles regarding the role of mission agencies with respect to local churches and the consequent downturn in giving to missions.

As examples of this discussion, in the *International Bulletin of Missionary Research* (October 1998), the lead article was "Local Churches vs. Traditional Mission Agencies" by Paul E. Pierson, and a companion article was "The Confusion of American Churches About Mission: A Response to Paul E. Pierson" by Paul Borthwick.[1] The titles of the articles speak for themselves.

James F. Engel in his book *A Clouded Future? Advancing North American World Missions*[2] reports there is an unmistakable downward trend [in financial giving to missions], that is likely to intensify no matter what we do in the way of public relations and marketing firepower. Engel also said, commenting on the results of a study by John and Sylvia Ronsvalle, "Two-thirds of pastors agreed that global missions is in sharp decline as a focus of today's church."

The reader may feel that these authors are discussing the past, but at the time this book went to press, the trends have not changed. My hope is that this book will contribute toward unprecedented missionary activity (helping counter the predicted trend) deep into the twenty-first century. That may be a tall order, but we are dealing with a foundational and fundamental part of missions: the individual missionary raising support.

The focus in this book is on the missionary. I believe that no matter what happens in the broader arena, the individual missionary will continue to play a significant role in shaping missions in the twenty-first century. I believe God will continue to call and send out individuals as His primary means of reaching the world. Many of these individuals and families will link up with mission agencies. Some will go out under the umbrella of larger churches that believe they have the means to handle the complexities of sending and sustaining missionaries on the field.

It's my expectation that if individual missionaries change some of their thinking about how they are doing missions, particularly support raising, they could change the *Clouded Future?* outcome the current discussion predicts. Note the question mark in the title of Engel's book.

And while the discussion is going on and the future being shaped, a goal of this book is to help change what is happening in the lives of many missionaries, right now.

I would like to see the quality of some missionaries' lives improve. But wait, aren't missionaries expected to live in poverty, and to sacrifice all for the cause?

Missionaries are expected to take risks, and to face the possibilities of sacrifice and suffering, but I think it is presumptuous to place life and limb in jeopardy as a result of deliberate failure to generate and maintain a complete network of prayer and financial partners.

Should quality of life even be an issue for a missionary? I believe it should be an issue. *"The laborer IS worthy of his hire"* (Luke 10:7 [emphasis mine]).

If for no other reason, the rising costs of being a missionary should cause everyone to realize financing a missionary is no trifling matter.

Missionaries can no longer just leave all and go. Realistically, they never could. Those who did, often paid a heavy, and unnecessary price. That part of the story comes later.

For the Tzeltal [Selltall] people of Mexico, buying a machete is a very important decision. Machetes must serve long and well. A machete is used to cut brush to clear fields, even small trees. It is used to cut grass and cane for building and roofing materials for Tzeltal houses. An inferior tool is rejected. Only a blade of good steel will do.

At the market where implements are usually purchased, a Tzeltal man chooses a machete from available stock. The buyer places his thumbnail on the blade, and plucks the blade just like plucking the string of a guitar. If he hears the ring of good steel, the ring of truth, he knows it will do the job, and do it for a long time. He puts down a week's wages.

Job expresses it differently than the Tzeltal, *"Just as my mouth can taste good food, so my mind tastes truth when I hear it."* (Job 12:11, Living Bible). But Job and the Tzeltal discovered the same thing about truth: truth produces a recognized sensory response.

We know truth when we taste it. We know truth when we hear it.

Sometimes truth is hard to find. I've been dedicated to finding all of the truth I can about raising support. It isn't as easy as choosing a machete. But if you know how to choose a machete, or recognize quality food, you will also have discovered an important characteristic of all truth: it sounds right; it tastes good.

Read this book actively; listen for the ring of truth. I trust you will not regret your purchase, and that it will leave a lasting, good taste.

Paul Johnson

END NOTES

[1] Paul E. Pierson, *Local Churches in Mission: What's Behind the Impatience with Traditional Mission Agencies?* and Paul Borthwick, *The Confusion of American Churches About Mission: A Response to Paul E. Pierson,* International Bulletin of Missionary Research, Gerald H. Anderson, ed., Vol. 22, No. 4, October 1998, pp. 146 and 151.

[2] James F. Engel, *A Clouded Future? Advancing North American World Missions, A Study of Parachurch Financing,* Underwritten by the Lilly Endowment, Inc., Wesley K. Willmer, Project Director and Editor-In-Chief, Milwaukee, Wisconsin, Christian Stewardship Association, 1996, p. 11. Engel has been the leading researcher and writer on church/missions issues for several years. Engel first came to my attention through his publication Averting the Financial Crisis in Christian Organizations: Insights from a Decade of Donor Research, Management Development Associates, 1983.

CHAPTER ONE

Failing at Faith— One Man's Story

Personal experience—though not always pleasant—can fuel the engine of creative work. I'm telling my story for this reason: because it will speak to some hurting hearts out there in the missionary community, and by God's grace will help to heal. Some of my workshop participants, when finding out I was going to write this book, specifically said, *"Make sure your story is included!"* My experience is the crucible within which this book was born.

Telling how God turned a most discouraging and frustrating experience into a deep-down soul search—mine—resulting in a time of confession, tears, and understanding, is not something I looked forward to putting in print. My story, however, has been a blessing to a lot of people and will serve as a backdrop against which we can explore the issues brought out in the later chapters of this book.

Let's start with an event I will never forget.

It was a prayer; a prayer God took twelve years to answer; a prayer I had totally forgotten. I was a new Christian stationed in the Philippines; about to be discharged from the Navy. Onmy knees at my bunk, I prayed: "Oh Lord, give me the opportunity to get the Gospel to all of those people who don't have it."

Twelve years later, I was standing on the doorstep of our house in Southern California, saying to a mission administrator, "Yes, we will be in Mexico next August to help run the school system for missionary kids." I was startled by an instantaneous recall—the recall of that prayer that had gone from my memory.

"Paul, I just answered your prayer."

As the administrator drove away, my thoughts returned to that twelve-year-old prayer. It was one of those existential moments. God said to my spirit, "Paul, I just answered your prayer!"

Wow, I thought, God just confirmed that he really does want us to be in missions. He did answer! He answered a prayer I had forgotten.

That prayer was motivated by finding God's Word to be the joy of my own life. Feeling that the Scriptures seemed to have been written just for me—God's love letter to me—I wanted to share this love.

Within weeks of receiving the Lord Jesus as my Savior, I learned about missions from missionaries right there in the Philippines. Their challenging lives and message drew me to the cause of reaching the world with the Gospel. And that's why I got down on my knees at my bunk one night and prayed, "Lord, let me help!"

"Lord, let me help!"

Imagine the excitement! My wife Dona and I, along with our two young sons, were going to be missionaries. We were going to help reach the world! God had, in a special way, put his seal on our decision.

How do you get started being a missionary? When it's a *faith mission,* somewhere in the early stages you start thinking about money. You have to start thinking about money.

We wouldn't receive a salary. We had to raise our own support. I have to admit I was in a fog about what it meant to raise support. No one I talked to seemed to know quite how to do it, but it was *by faith*. So having known quite a number of faith missionaries and having heard and read a lot of stories, all of which implied it all works out somehow, I felt it would work out for us too.

And you know what? At first it seemed to work out just as everyone said it would. We talked to our pastor and to several friends. We wrote some letters. We set a date.

If by that date we had 80% of our monthly support pledged I would resign from my teaching position. In 1972, 80% of our budget was $600 per month. It happened. So we left for the mission field.

Ten years later, after a long struggle with finances, I had to face the reality of insufficient support, a reality about which I had been in denial.

I will never forget the day it all began to unravel.

It should have been a great day. My department was fulfilling its goals in various places around the world. Besides, it was a beautiful day in Southern California, you know, the endless summer.

It wasn't, however, a beautiful day in my spirit. There was a black cloud hanging around, represented by a folded, stapled document lying on the corner of my desk. Our monthly financial statement had been delivered that morning.

It was there all day long, unopened.

Financial statements are a record of the debits and credits in a missionary's account for the previous month. Credits represent the money coming in from financial partners, and debits are the costs of being a self-employed missionary: Social Security, retirement, medical and life insurance, etc. Back then, a check from our agency for our month's support was wrapped up inside the monthly financial report. The check was for what was left over each month; the money that remained to live on.

"I'll never forget the day it began to unravel."

Our financial situation had become distressing to me, actually depressing, almost debilitating. We were in debt to the organization (a red account), and receiving less than one-half each month of what our full budget required. I just couldn't open those financial statements anymore. So there it sat—a black cloud of doom hanging over my day.

I took the unopened financial statements home to Dona. She always had the courage to open them. (Dona says it wasn't "courage," just the reality someone had to open them.) It was me who didn't have the courage. The amount of those checks was getting less and less. It was like adding another turn of the screw, every month, to the pressure I felt.

Dona was at the stove when I walked in. I put the financial statement on the kitchen table and waited. Eventually Dona turned around, sat down, and opened it. In a few moments she looked at me.

With her tears dropping on that check, she said, "Paul, it's for twenty dollars."

Something broke inside of me. I tell you this with hindsight. At the time, I didn't even understand what was going on. I got up from the table and walked toward the back of the house. I was screaming in my spirit, screaming at God.

Don't you know we are faith missionaries?

Don't you see my wife's tears? Don't you know I can't feed my children? Don't you know I can't even pay the rent? Don't you know I can't provide for my children, my wife? Why aren't you providing?

Don't you know we are faith missionaries?

I didn't tell Dona what was going on inside of me. I think I was in a state of spiritual shock.

The feelings of defeat and self-pity overwhelmed me. I was shocked at my anger towards God. I can't remember ever, up to that time in twenty-five years as a Christian, being angry with

God. And oh, the anger that became bitterness, that became mistrust which was like a lingering poison—debilitating, sapping strength, and, in a way, killing me. I did consider taking my life. Anger turned inward does that. (I'm crying as I write this.)

Somehow these memories still linger, not as poison, but as a kind of spiritual memorial.

"Put thou my tears in thy bottle" (Psalm 56:8, KJV)

What were we to do? What was *I* going to do? Dona went to work to pay the rent and to put food on the table. I started driving a school bus part-time. It took two years to become solvent. It was not a happy time.

Dona and I were both expected to work in the ministry—Dona at least part-time, and me full-time. We wanted to and felt guilty we couldn't. We felt guilty even though we had talked it over with an administrator and had permission to work outside the organization.

All this time God had been planning something. In the midst of the darkest time of my life, God was working.

I had a good friend in our mission, the director of one of the home-country programs. I had confided in him some of my feelings. He was a good listener—I was to learn how good.

About the time the debts were being finally cleared, my friend, as they say, "threw me a curve." And what a curve! He wanted me to come to work in his office, and to start a new position.

"He wanted me to help other missionaries raise their support!"

He wanted *me* to help other missionaries raise their support!

You can sense just how ridiculous that was. I told him so, but he persisted. He asked me to pray about it. For some reason the Lord seemed to be saying to me, "Do it." I didn't tell God He was ridiculous, but I did tell Him I couldn't understand why He would want me to take such a job. I could not imagine a less-qualified person. Didn't He remember? We still didn't have adequate support. And of course, I had no idea how to help other missionaries. I didn't even know how to help myself. It all seemed highly unusual to me, which I did tell the Lord.

"It's always too soon to quit."

Why didn't we quit? All I can say is that God wouldn't let us.

I felt like the pilot and gas stove repairman I heard about.

The pilot's engine conked out; he bailed out; the parachute didn't open. While he was falling toward the earth, he noticed a man coming up. As they were passing in the air, the pilot yelled to the man who was coming up, "Hey, do you know anything about parachutes?"

"No," he answered, "and I don't know anything about gas stoves, either!"

I felt helpless. I didn't know how to raise support, or what to tell anyone else. I took the position.

As has been said by many other fellow travelers in their experiences with God, He finally had me where he wanted me.

Where was I? At a very clean desk—not much to do when you don't know anything. So I prayed.

I still remember my actual prayer, a prayer arising from some moments of realizing, even in a deeper way than before, the reason I didn't know what to do for anyone else was because I didn't know what to do for myself. Why is it finances have been such a frustrating area of my life, our lives, I wondered? Those moments of wondering turned into this prayer.

"Lord, if you will show me what's wrong with me, I'll try to help other missionaries."

"LORD, if you will show me what's wrong with me, I'll try to help other missionaries."

Have you ever asked God to show you what's wrong in some area of your life? I don't recommend it! Unless you're serious. By God's grace, I was. It was seriousness driven by desperation.

When I was growing up, my dad used to say to us kids, "If you don't straighten up we're going out behind the woodshed." Sometimes we didn't even have a woodshed, but no matter, we all knew what Dad meant. God knew about the woodshed too. He took my prayer seriously, and to the woodshed we went.

What did I learn? Well, it's rather complex because there were some deep emotional and behavioral things that began to surface. You see, God began to show me some deeply ingrained, debilitating attitudes. The following illustration helped me to understand how serious these attitudes really were. I'll share the illustration, and then make some applications.

When the U.S. launches a ship and crew into space, the success of the voyage depends upon the ship keeping a proper attitude. Attitude, in space travel, is a composite concept. The pitch, roll, and yaw has to be controlled to maintain proper attitude. If for some reason the attitude (the direction and position of the ship in relation to points of reference, and in relation to the target destination) of the ship is faulty, the crew and ship could be lost in space, they would miss their target. It's really important to note that the reference points (earth, another planet, a star) are very significant in maintaining proper flight attitude. It's also important to know that an internal guidance system in the space craft monitors the ship's attitude and corrects the course relative to these points of reference.

Now if a missionary's attitudes (please accept the pluralization of attitude, for illustration's sake) are faulty, he will also miss the target, in this case, by application, full financial support. Attitudes are critical.

So, out behind the woodshed, God began to expose some attitudes that had been causing me to miss the target. It seemed as if each attitude, as it came to light, was like receiving a good WHACK from the paddle.

In case you were wondering, God does know how to use the paddle.

I'll tell you about some of my faulty attitudes.

J.I. Packer, talks about sin-bred unrealism.

"To live wisely, you have to be clear-sighted and realistic—ruthlessly so—in looking at life as it is. Wisdom will not go with comforting illusions, false sentiment, or the use of rose-colored spectacles. Most of us live in a dream world, with our heads in the clouds and our feet off the ground; we never see the world, and our lives in it, as they really are. This deep-seated, sin-bred unrealism is one reason why there is so little wisdom among us—even the soundest and most orthodox of us."[1]

There it is: unrealism—an attitude, a faulty attitude, a sin.

If the missionary's reference points are faulty—faulty understanding, missing or over-influential reference point, or something is wrong in the internal guidance system—bad judgment, poor training and preparation, etc., the missionary's attitude(s) will be skewed and the target missed.

How can a missionary be unrealistic about finances? Well, one way is to make the decision to leave for the field with only 80% support. I made that decision. The problem wasn't just that we only had 80% pledged, but we had to also cover all outgoing expenses, travel, and first-month living expenses. We had used up our savings; and income from support wouldn't start until after we got to our assignment. Well, when you're going by faith, these questions—issues—have an easy solution: God will provide.

What would happen if, in this tenuous financial condition, financial partners had to drop out? What if it were a major loss like $300 per month?

That is exactly what happened!

Remember our 80% budget was $600 per month. We might have weathered the storm if we had had full financial support. We didn't. It was unrealistic to sell our home, all of our furniture, withdraw all of my school system retirement, and use all of these monies to try to finance our going with only 80% support pledged. Yet that is what I did.

• • • • • • • • 14 • • • • • • • • • • • • • • • • • • •

By the way, Dona asked me a lot of wise questions about these decisions. I wasn't listening. I had my cliches ready: "God will take care of us. We're going to live by faith. I don't know how it will be done, but God will provide."

Let me tell you what I did about the problem of losing half of our financial support. Nothing. Oh, yes, I did pray. Why didn't I do something else? Because I was very passive about financial things.

Once, in an evening service, a member of the audience asked me, "Hey, we know you are faith missionaries. How are you doing?" I answered, "Things are going great, we're trusting God."

What a misrepresentation of the truth. It was actually a lie. Things were not going great. Our financial situation was not only bad, but deteriorating. But I had such a passive attitude about finances, I couldn't speak the truth.

"It was a lie!"

Let me say, too, parenthetically, that to admit lack of support would have been, in my thinking at the time, admitting my lack of faith, or leaving the possibility open that God was unhappy with me. Perhaps there was some unresolved sin in my life.

I couldn't tell anyone about our financial needs, even when asked.

To tell anyone other than God about our financial needs would have been a violation of what I believed; it would have violated my conscience, and as I've said, an admission of spiritual failure. Extreme, I know, but nevertheless, true.

But there it was, another attitude, passivity. There was a reason behind this, but that comes later.

We are taught in the Bible to be *"Not slothful in business; fervent in spirit; serving the Lord"* (Romans 12:11, KJV). I had a slothful attitude. WHACK!

I kept no records of what was happening to us financially. I didn't know who gave, or how much, or when. Sloth, defined by any dictionary comes out as laziness, or lack of exertion. This was a particularly hard whack in that I worked hard all of my life. Why wasn't I working at the business of being a missionary? Well, for one thing, I never believed it required work, or that it had a business aspect to it. If God is providing, it's His business.

The WHACKS by now were coming regularly. You probably will have trouble believing this, but as a missionary I never planned ahead, financially. I took it a day (in reality a month) at a time. You see, my attitude was that I didn't have to plan for financial things. God would provide. It would be wrong to plan ahead. It wouldn't be living by faith.

I remember one time, in Mexico, when we didn't even have money to buy food or take the kids to a doctor, which they needed. Dona told me about the situation. I said, "Hey, honey, the Lord will provide." She asked me how I thought we would pay for food, rent, and other necessities the next month, not to mention the need for a doctor. I didn't know, but somehow the Lord would miraculously meet our needs, was my response.

He didn't.

By now you are probably concluding that I was pretty dumb, or very irresponsible. I was both. WHACK! WHACK!

Early in the experience I'm describing to you, I started blaming God for our troubles. It was clear. God was failing me.

"There it was, indelibly tatooed on my spiritual backside, irresponsibility."

But it became clearer and clearer, out there behind the woodshed, who was *really* responsible, and who was failing. In fact, what came through with one of those whacks was the deep sense of my being highly irresponsible. It hurt. It was the same feeling I had when considering the issue of slothfulness. All my life I've been known as a responsible person. Irresponsibility was a difficult attitude for me to acknowledge. But there it was, indelibly tattooed on my spiritual backside, irresponsibility.

The hardest attitude to deal with was yet to come. It goes

back to Dona's tears at the kitchen table. I don't remember Dona ever crying about our financial situation before (in ten years she had had plenty of opportunity and reason to cry). It may have been her tears that pushed me into my reaction of blaming God, etc. I don't know. But what I do know is that she had been carrying a heavy load for those ten years, a load I was oblivious to.

When we first went to Mexico, I had it all figured out. I was the one with the ministry. Dona would take care of our two boys (three months and four years), do all of the correspondence, be mother and wife-of-the-year, and take care of the finances, all the while living in a different culture with a language we didn't speak well. I don't like admitting all this; but that was my attitude.

In our first ten years as missionaries, I never wrote one letter: newsletter or personal letter. I had the attitude that it was all Dona's responsibility. After all, she's a better writer and speaker. It's just natural she should handle those things. How convenient for me.

I think by now you are seeing the pattern: an irresponsible, slothful, passive, and shortsighted husband and father. But why? Well, fundamentally, my faulty attitudes were the result of an ideology I had bought into.

Bierstedt defines an ideology as a combination of *idea* and *norm*. Norms are *ways of doing things* in a culture. In my case, the faith mission's culture. *Norms are standards, rules, and expectations.* More precisely, an ideology is an idea supported by a norm. We are encouraged to believe it, not because it is true, but because such belief is regarded as right and proper in our society. Further, *ideologies are the ideas…we are required to believe if we wish to remain in good standing in our social groups.*[2]

At the heart, an ideology consists of a basic idea (rule/standard/law) that is held to by a given group. When a group agrees to operate by that idea it becomes a norm: a rule of behavior for

"We are encouraged to believe it, not because it is true, but because such belief is regarded as right and proper in our society."

anyone wanting to be accepted by that group. The combination
—idea adopted as norm—produces the ideology.

With that insight, it became clear to me that living by faith
was, for me, really an ideology.

It isn't very far from ideology to idol!

*Let us beware lest we in our pride accept the erroneous notion
that idolatry consists only in kneeling before visible objects of adora-
tion, and that civilized peoples are therefore free from it. The essence
of idolatry is the entertainment of thoughts about God that are unworthy of Him.* A.W. Tozer[3]

Idolatry, then, is the entertainment of wrong thoughts about
God.

Throughout the experience I've been relating to you, there
were many wrong thoughts about God. One of the reasons for
those wrong thoughts was a deeply held ideology that pointed
to the conclusion: God is responsible for this!

Ideologies must have a means of expression. There must be
a way of stating the ideology in working terms: operational terms.
Bierstedt uses the word *technique* to define this feature of an
ideology. In faith missions, technique is expressed in these ways:
*Tell God only; Go into your closet and pray; God provides; Trust
God; It's by faith; Never tell your financial needs; etc.*

Exposing attitudes (showing me what I really was) and showing me the source of these attitudes, had a purpose. It was all
leading somewhere. I didn't know where. I didn't even know I
was being led. Only God could take a mess like what I've been
describing and create something of value.

*"Happy and fortunate is the man whom God reproves; so do not
despise or reject the correction of the Almighty [subjecting you to trial
and suffering]. For He wounds, but He binds up; He smites, but His
hands heal"* (Job 5:17–18, The Amplified Old Testament).

How does God "bind up?" How do "his hands heal?" The
Lord is a good doctor—washing the wounds, applying the right

IDEOLOGY

IDOLATRY

"Only God could take a
mess like what I've
been describing
and create something
of value."

medication, binding them. What means does God use for this spiritual service to an inflicted heart? *That he might sanctify and cleanse it with the washing of water by the word* (Ephesians 5:26, KJV).

It was the washing of the Word that brought healing. It didn't happen overnight. The answers began to come as I started asking these questions: "How did I get these attitudes? Where did they come from?"

Well, it was clear to me that these attitudes were the fruit of a way of thinking. In fact, I said to myself, I must not really understand this thing of living by faith. I must be missing some important scriptural truth. Otherwise, how could I have gotten so messed up?

So, I set about studying the Bible.

My initial goal was to find the doctrine—the teaching—of living by faith. The second goal was to correct my understanding so that I could start seeing God bless us financially. I wanted to know how to live by faith. I wanted it to work for me like it seemed to for everyone else.

The shocker came (after hours of study) when I began to realize the Bible presented a different picture about the financial support of Christian workers than I had ever imagined.

There was another shocker: in the midst of this self-discovery, I was finding out there were quite a number of missionaries for whom living by faith wasn't working, either. Remember my friend who had asked me to help other missionaries? By now I was trying and discovering how widespread the problem was.

I was searching through these things myself, and at the same time trying to help missionaries who needed to work on their financial support. I was looking into the Scriptures for answers and looking into the historical foundations of faith missions, and the ideology of living by faith.

While working at the daily business of being a support-raising consultant, I talked to a lot of people.

All of this self-discovery, Bible study, and historical study led me to begin developing the biblical/philosophical/practical foundations for a support-raising program. What is presented in the remaining chapters comes out of real life and work.

The process took several years, and there was a lot of help.

This book from here on is in a developmental flow: from foundational concepts like *Living by Faith: Myth and Reality; Living by Faith: The Test of Scripture, Biblical Precedents, Patterns, and Principles: The Triumph of Scripture, the Partnership Model* (which requires two chapters and is the second major section), and *Getting Clear on the Concepts*. The last chapters in the third section focus on practical ideas and suggestions.

The author has something to say, which he perceives to be true and useful, or helpfully beautiful. So far as he knows, no one has yet said it; so far as he knows, no one else can say it. He is bound to say it, clearly and melodiously if he may; clearly, at all events. In the sum of his life he finds this to be the thing, or group of things, manifest to him—this, the piece of true knowledge, or sight, which his share of sunshine and earth has permitted him to seize. He would fain set it down forever; engrave it on the rock, if he could, saying, "This is the best of me; ...this, if anything of mine, is worth your memory."[4]

Part of *my* memory has to do with the history of the movement called Independent Faith Missions. It began over one hundred and fifty years ago, and has had a dominating impact on the belief systems of thousands of missionaries.

The faith mission ideology had a dominating impact on me. I wanted to be a man of God. The first two books I read were *Hudson Taylor's Spiritual Secrets* and *George Müeller, Man of Faith*.

If their lives and teachings were what it meant to be a man of God, well, that was what I wanted.

My attraction to this ideology was doubly powerful because

I come from a nonreligious background. Religious teaching and experience were nonexistent in my upbringing. I had nothing to weigh the ideology against.

Listen for the ring of truth as we explore some of the history of the living by faith ideology, particularly the aspect of financially living by faith.

END NOTES

[1] J.I. Packer, *Knowing God*, Downers Grove, InterVarsity Press, 1973, p. 93.

[2] Robert Bierstedt, *The Social Order: An Introduction to Sociology*, New York, McGraw-Hill Book Company, Inc. 1957, pp.137-153.

[3] A.W. Tozer, *The Knowledge of the Holy*, New York, Harper and Row, 1961, p. 11

[4] Ruskin, John, *Sesame and Lillies*, Project Guttenburg, Release #1293 (April 1998).

CHAPTER TWO
• • • • • • • • •

Living By Faith
Myth and Reality

The great enemy of the truth is very often not the lie, deliberate, contrived and dishonest, but the myth—persistent, persuasive and unrealistic. —John F. Kennedy

It is a serious decision to become a missionary. It's particularly serious if one chooses to join a mission agency that doesn't pay a salary, or provide benefits: life insurance, medical insurance, retirement, etc. It gets more serious when a person or couple decide to take on this challenge for a lifetime: to be a career missionary.

A missionary's budget in today's market is a major challenge. A single person going to an overseas assignment will need somewhere between $2000 to $2500 per month, plus or minus, but more than likely, plus. A couple? Probably between $2500 and $3000. A family of four: $3500 to $4000, but if schooling for children is a budget item, you can quickly get to $5000 per month, and beyond. Some home assignments, and some overseas assignments require more per month than the above figures indicate.

A family of four going to Latin America in 1972 had a budget of only $700 per month. What will it cost tomorrow?

Missionaries can count on an annual escalation depending upon such things as inflation, a child added to the family, expansion of ministry, change of assignment location, tax increases, additional training and education, etc., and there will be the loss of some partners along the way (attrition).

In addition to regular monthly needs there is the **set-up budget**: the need for thousands of dollars for travel, housing costs, and equipment, like a vehicle, computer, etc.

This is no time for myths. It's a time to be sure of one's footing. It's time for reality.

"This is no time for myths."

The chapter, *One Man's Story,* was my story: how I tried to base my family's material well-being on the ideology living by faith. The confusion and negative experiences were a result of not being able to sort out myth from reality.

Reality was fogged in by myth.

Is it only one missionary who has been confused, uncertain, and stifled? In seminars and workshops on the subject of raising support, missionaries—young and old, entry level and veteran—often say:

> *"Going through this workshop was the turning point for me."*
> *"Everyone in our organization should have this training, where have you been?"*
> *"Your outlook on support was refreshing and gave me a whole new perspective on support raising."*
> *"The workshop transformed my whole outlook. I can go forward now with the confidence this is God's way."*
> *"Why wasn't I told this twenty years ago!"*

There are a lot of stuck people. How stuck?

Jim, a family man, a missionary, a son of missionaries, was discouraged with his financial situation. It wasn't clear just how discouraged Jim was. He had been exposed to some of the ideas in this book. But Jim found he just couldn't take the actions these ideas suggested.

The financial struggle continued for a few years. The struggle and confusion made no sense until Jim had an opportunity to talk with his dad. Jim said, "I had just returned from a long trip visiting friends and family. While visiting with my dad, I told him how difficult it was for us, financially. I told Dad the philosophy he had taught me wasn't working. I told him I needed to do something differently.

"Son, I wish I had done it differently...."

"Dad responded, 'Son, I wish I had done it differently too. Go ahead. Do what you think is right.'"

Jim said at that very moment he felt a sense of relief, of freedom. He realized he had been stuck in his father's belief system. Jim hadn't been able to be very active in raising support because he had been raised with a philosophy "God provides, just pray." He certainly couldn't tell anyone about his financial needs. And it was one of the most important people in his life who had passed this belief along. Jim concluded,

"And HE HAD TO release me...."

"I had to be released from my father's beliefs, and he had to release me."

How does it happen that a missionary can be so unrealistic about financial matters? Get so stuck?

To put it simply, you believe the stories. What stories? Stories told by missionaries when they stand in front of churches that support them, or that are written in newsletters to the missionary's constituency. It's the stories highlighting some miraculous provision of God. It's the story that says, "Yesterday, we needed $129.89, and today a check came for $129.89 from someone we didn't even know, and who couldn't have known about our need. It was a miracle!"

The same missionary who relates a story like that usually fails to tell about how the money comes to pay the rent month after month, or to pay the food bill, buy clothes for the kids, put gas in the car, etc., month-after-month. Miracle stories tend to obscure the reality of daily/monthly life.

In reality, there isn't a miracle story for every financial need. Miracles are few and far between for most missionaries. Missionaries actually depend upon the money, usually received on a monthly basis, that comes regularly, from the missionary's network of church and individual financial partners.

Some stories become legendary and are memorialized in books sold in the Christian marketplace. Miracle stories coming from the realm of faith missions tend to grow to mythological proportions. Miracle stories tend to dominate reality.

I don't discount or deny the stories of miraculous provision. I could tell some of my own. I do deny that miracles, prayer alone, and extraordinary faith are the total truth upon which a missionary's material well-being should rest, or does rest.

If you were to engage a dedicated faith missionary, Jim for example, in a discussion of why and how it came about that he accepted and attempted to practice the ideology living by faith, he would undoubtedly bring up the names of at least one of these three people: William Carey, Hudson Taylor, or George Müller, besides his dad.

Modern faith missions rests upon the premise of faith alone, (telling no one but God of your financial needs) which originated with, grew out of, and became popularized from the speaking, writing, and promotion of Müller, and Taylor.

Actually, there were other speakers and writers who popularized, overly dramatized and spiritualized what Müller and Taylor did and said that produced the ideology. In the process, the tales have grown in the telling and out of all proportion to the day-by-day experience of those who adopted the live-by-faith model. If Müller and Taylor knew what has been propagated and promoted in their names they might, as the saying goes, "turn over in their graves."

What does it mean to *live by faith?* One peculiarity of this ideology is that it applies mostly to the realm of financial provi-

"We remember a time of threatened famine, when prices were suddenly rising and £20 was needed to lay in a stock of paddy (unshelled rice). That week brought us a single gift of £20 from a friend in England, whose very name up to that time was unknown to us."[1]

"Miracle stories tend to obscure and dominate reality."

sion. It means missionaries depend on the voluntary gifts of God's people, but ask only God, never ask God's people. Going by faith means you may be going with God, and with no one else. This seems very spiritual.

This ideology has had disastrous effects for some missionaries. The New York Independent in 1899 had this editorial:

"For some time reports have been coming to this office of suffering on the part of missionaries sent out by.... They have come from widely separate countries and from people in whose judgment and fairness we have every confidence. One told the story of a young man of fine character and earnest devotion, left without support in a country where it was impossible for him to secure assistance, and who sickened, became insane, and took his own life. Another told of not merely one, but several who had been left similarly deserted, had suffered greatly with sickness in consequence, and life had been saved only by the relief furnished by missionaries of other mission boards. Similar letters have been received by others. All have been accompanied with an urgent request for investigation of the management of the Society, and the exposure of the methods which have resulted in such cruelties. Every effort was rendered difficult by the peculiar character of the Society. It takes no pledge of support for its missionaries, simply promises to distribute among them whatever funds are committed to it."[2]

The popular radio speaker Paul Harvey usually divides stories into two segments. He uses the catchy phrase, "The rest of the story" to introduce the audience to the second segment and to alert the audience that now he will tell what really happened.

"The myth got out of hand."

Keeping in mind the date of publication of the above newspaper story, the rest of the story of faith missions has rarely been told. It needs to be told. The myth has gotten out of hand.

Almost everyone acquainted with missions knows William Carey is referred to as the "Father of modern missions." His famous quote, "Attempt great things for God; expect great things from God" still resounds in many missionary publications.

William Carey was the most prolific linguist and Bible translator the church has known. His prodigious output in India is still praised in the annals of Bible translation.

His financial needs in India were met by employment, first in an Indigo factory, and later as a professor. Carey was called a faith missionary, but at the time of his going to India the term "faith missions" didn't include the concept, "tell God only about financial needs, and depend only on God for financial needs."

For his time, by the definition of his time, Carey did fit under the umbrella of what was then known as faith missions. But he doesn't fit under the George Müller/Hudson Taylor definition of faith missions.

George Müller of Bristol is probably the most often-quoted person when it comes to the ideology, living by faith. He, in fact, set the stage for Hudson Taylor and many other missionaries and mission societies (agencies). It was the Müller/Taylor mix that brought into faith missions the idea/norm/ideology, tell God only about your financial needs.

Müller is notable for his ministry to orphans. He is notable for the many specific, timely answers to prayer resulting in funds, food, and shelter for thousands of British orphans. He had a great heart for missions and gave much to missions. Hudson Taylor and the China Inland Mission directly benefitted from his fund-raising, and his personal interest.

George Müller claimed that he never told anyone but God about his financial needs. In reality, through forms of public communication, including many opportunities to speak in churches and regular newsletters to his constituency, the needs of the orphanages were constantly kept before the public. But more than that, Müller often spoke on the subject of living by faith and challenged people to give, by faith. He told and wrote stories about past giving to promote further giving.

Dwight L. Moody said about Müller, "His emphasis on 'making no appeals was itself an appeal!'"[3]

How did it actually work? In the early years of Müller's ministry it didn't work.

From Müller's diary:

Aug. 18—"I have not one penny in hand."

Aug. 31—"I have been waiting on the Lord for means—but as yet the Lord has not been pleased to send help."

Sept. 11—"The Good Lord in His wisdom still sees it useful to keep us very low."[4]

This pattern went on for a few years.

It wasn't until he began speaking and publishing that the wave of interest and giving began to move with a powerful surge bringing funds into the ministry of the orphanages. Müller's stories of how God miraculously met needs fueled interest and financial response.

Müller said in an interview, "Seven million five hundred thousand dollars have been sent to me in answer to prayer. We have needed as much as two hundred thousand dollars in one year, and it has all come when needed. No man can ever say I asked him for a penny. We have no committees, no collectors, no voting, and no endowment. All has come in answer to believing prayer."[5]

Müller's prayer life, and faith, cannot be doubted, but when we see, as have others, significant efforts to communicate the needs of the orphanages, significant efforts to tell of how God met the needs (miraculous stories appeal to the emotions and the pocketbook), and significant efforts in preaching and teaching from the pulpit, and in written publications, to challenge

Christians to give, we have to conclude a substantial myth built up around these anecdotes.

Müller did more than tell God alone, as those who promoted the myth would have us believe. It wasn't until Müller began to publicize and promote the orphanages that money began flowing in. The flow of money was as much from the activities of Müller in reaching out to the community—the worldwide community—with the needs of the orphanages, as it was from his prayers.

And what a community it was. It was the era of the great revivals sweeping England and the United States, a second and third wave of what is sometimes called the "Great Awakening." It was a time of unprecedented church growth, giving, and missionary sending. It is estimated that during those years Müller travelled and told his stories in at least forty-two countries.

In the twentieth-century missionary community, it was not well-known that Müller published in the local paper the names of donors with the amounts of money they gave (a powerful marketing principle). He invited people to come to the orphanages to pray, and conveniently placed offering baskets near the door of the orphanages. To say Müller never asked for money is a zealous overstatement.

There are indications Müller himself did not personally rely upon the faith-alone method for his personal funds as his wife's family was the source of considerable financial contribution. It is reported that he kept his own personal funds separate from the operational budget of the orphanages. [10]

Müller was not a missionary, but he had a deep interest in missions, helped send missionaries, and was a great blessing to Hudson Taylor. Müller made at least two trips to China to personally carry funds to Taylor's work.

It was Müller's public speaking, writing, and personal interest in missions that had attracted the attention of Hudson Tay-

It must be conceded that the life which George Müller led at Bristol was a beautiful life of faith and devotion, but the history of religion has shown again and again that such a life may be quite consistent with honest mistakes in principle. He possessed a rare personal magnetism, and won many friends wherever he went and whithersoever his circulars and reports were sent. But it was felt, from the first, by many observers of his work that while he definitely eschewed all appeals for money, yet indirectly the publications which he issued were the most effective of all appeals. [8]

"When I got out to China, I thought to myself, I shall have no claim on anyone for anything. My only claim will be on God. How important to learn, before leaving England, to move man, through God, by prayer alone." [9]

29

"Practically the missionaries will depend for support on the voluntary gifts of God's people, But the asking must not be of the people but of God: the contribution box must give place to prayer."[11]

"Usually, the 1858-'59 revival is seen as the one succeeding the Great Awakening, but there was another revival between the two, in the 1830s which, although less impressive and less widespread, produced three movements which would strongly influence the revival of 1858-'59 and, with it, faith missions: the holiness movement, the Brethren movement, and the Prophetic movement. In faith mission circles, the succession of revivals is usually seen to have stopped with the 1858-'59 revival and its second wave in 1873.[12]

lor. The live-by-faith principle was particularly attractive to Taylor. Taylor was to become the standard bearer of the ideology of living by faith for the modern missionary movement, known as "Faith Missions."

Taylor, before going to China, tested his faith in the slums of Hull, England. It was deliberate on his part. He wanted to know if he had enough faith at home before attempting to trust God on the mission field.

Reading of his personal sacrifices and his ministry in an economically deprived area, one cannot help but admire his walk with the Lord, and his personal integrity in working through the issue of trust in the Lord alone for provision. The book, *Hudson Taylor's Spiritual Secrets*, written by his son and daughter-in-law, has blessed and inspired thousands of readers, including the author of this book.

As Taylor sought to test his readiness for going to China, he chose money as a medium for the test. For example, while working for a doctor he determined to never tell the doctor, even though the doctor was known for forgetting such things, when his salary was due.

But it was not really an issue of money to Taylor at that point, it was a test to see if he was ready for ministry in China.

On one occasion when the doctor forgot to pay his salary and Hudson was penniless and hungry, and praying, the doctor asked Taylor if in fact his salary wasn't due. Taylor, of course, said "Yes." Unfortunately the doctor had already sent his earnings into the bank. The doctor was disappointed that Taylor hadn't told him earlier. Taylor took his own disappointment to God in prayer.

A few hours later the doctor returned with money that a wealthy client, who normally didn't pay in this manner, had just given to pay his bill.

This kind of experience convinced Taylor he was ready to

go to China as a missionary. He passed his self-imposed test. He had enough faith proven in the financial domain. Subsequently, it was faith for finances that would become the guiding star of the faith-alone principle.

Taylor originally went to China under the auspices and ostensible support of the Chinese Evangelisation Society in China (CES). CES was supposed to have provided Taylor's financial support. Taylor had not yet fully adopted the faith-alone principle. However, the financial arrangement did not work well. Taylor, except for the kindness of a doctor and his wife who were already in China, would have been destitute because funds from CES never arrived in the early months.

Disagreements between Taylor and the Society developed. Four years later, Taylor broke with CES. It was in this general period when Müller became a benefactor and mentor to Taylor.

When Taylor formed the China Inland Mission (CIM) the policy was that no overt forms of soliciting funds were allowed. Thus, the term "faith mission" became popularized and identified with CIM as none of the CIM missionaries were allowed to raise money for support in a direct, personal way.

The phrase "full information, no solicitation" became the slogan to explain this unusual policy. They would depend on God alone for their finances.

But again, we must ask, isn't this an overstatement of the actual situation? What is "full information" if it is not solicitation? If examined closely, the statement full information, no solicitation reveals itself to be nothing more than an oxymoron: *a figure of speech in which opposite or contradictory ideas or terms are combined* (Webster's Dictionary)." How can one give full information and not be soliciting?

Faith missionaries have often expressed their needs in newsletters in ways similar to this: "Please pray for a serious financial need we have. Without the funds to go forward we will

The great amount of money needed... occasioned methods of raising funds which to some seemed mechanical. There arose thus in the minds of not a few a wish for less of routine, less of rule, more of spirit. The wonderful work of George Müller...had its effect, and men began to ask why missions might not be conducted on the same basis. These ideas were developed by the Reverend J. Hudson Taylor...."[13]

"The somewhat eccentric founder was imbued with consuming missionary fervor and inaugurated some radical methods, many of which have been corrected by experience.[14]

miss God's special opportunity to evangelize these people. The door may close any day. Pray with us for the needed funds!"

Is asking for prayer merely a euphemism to avoid asking for money? Could this be a form of spiritual self-deceit?

Taylor, back in England, having separated from the Society that first sent him to China, began publishing a missionary newsletter with the title "China's Millions."

Through this publication the Christian public, particularly in England, but also in the United States and in other parts of the world, was made aware of the needs of the ministry and given information on how to send donations. He published a pamphlet telling how monies could be bequeathed from estates to finance the mission. He published the names of people and amounts they gave. He had learned well from his mentor, George Müller.

Killion says, "Taylor learned another lesson from Müller; the power of the periodical." He goes on to ask, "Did the China Inland Mission (CIM) solicit funds? Not in conventional ways. Did they get the message out? Yes. Is that fund-raising? Here again the answer is suddenly not black or white. Two things are certain: first, the fund-raising policy of the CIM was not to go into the closet, shut the door, and pray and never tell anyone but God about their needs, and second, Hudson Taylor did a great work for God in China"[15]

In the book *Hudson Taylor and the China Inland Mission*, the authors relate an example of how a publication contributed to financial results for the CIM.

"That was the book [*China's Spiritual Need and Claims*] that did the work," said Mr. Stevenson, who was just home from Burma. At a single meeting five pounds' worth [the value of the books sold at that meeting] would be purchased. Many new friends were attached to the Mission as a result, and a constant stream of gifts poured in.[17]

One of the curious contradictions in the live-by-faith philosophy is that, in most cases, the mission organization is very active in fund-raising while the individual missionary is forbidden to use the same methods. "The organization can, but I can't" is a lament that can be heard among individual missionaries.

Müller and Taylor used public means of propagating their ministries and made it clear how people could help. Means were established for receiving funds from donors who, hearing of the destitute orphans and teeming millions of Chinese without the Gospel, were encouraged to give.

Are these methods consistent with the ideology of telling God only—living by faith alone—just pray and God will supply?

When we see that the Christian leaders who were identified with this philosophy were actually not practicing it, as they had intensive and extensive publicity campaigns to encourage giving to their respective ministries, the whole idea of telling God only shows itself for what it really is, a myth. They were really, as it were, telling the whole world.

However, these men and their wonderful lives of sacrifice, devotion to the causes they were respectively committed to, and their faith and personal walks with the Lord are not a myth.

What is the problem?

"Where the exercise of faith; in this particular use of the word, is employed mainly in one specific line, as for example, where the object in view is almost exclusively the receipt of money, there is danger that a doctrine of faith may be developed which will not endure the test of Scripture or sound experience."[19]

"**The test of Scripture.**" Should we test the ideology of living by faith against Scripture? If we want to be sure we are hearing the ring of truth, we will have to conduct the test. The

The Reality:
"In 1862 he returned to China with two associates, working on this basis [prayer alone]. It became evident, however, that there must be some medium for the transmission of funds and some organization for the selection of candidates.... It [CIM] continues to carry out the idea of simple faith and prayer, although it holds public meetings and issues regular reports."[18]

only way to know is to examine the texts of Scripture most often used to support the ideology.

Jesus said, *"You shall know the truth, and the truth shall set you free"* (John 8:32, KJV).

Come along and consider the most popular biblical passages used in defense of this ideology. Listen for the "ring of truth."

END NOTES

[1] Elizabeth Elliot, *A Chance to Die: The Life and Legacy of Amy Carmichael*, Fleming H. Revell, 1987 p. 189.

[2] Frank E. Ellinwood, D.D.L.L.D., *Questions and Phases of Modern Missions, Dodd, Mead and Company, 1899*, p. 148.

[3] Jim Killion, *George Muller and the Quest for Biblical Balance in Fundraising*, Dallas, Killion, McCabe and Associates, 1994, p. 10.

[4] Killion, *George Muller and the Quest*, p. 8.

[5] A. Sims, Editor, *George Muller Man of Faith*, Grand Rapids, Zondervan Publishing House, 1892, p. 7.

[6] Killion, *George Muller and the Quest*, p. 10.

[7] E.M. Bliss, D.D., *A Concise History of Missions*, Chicago, Fleming H. Revell, 1897, p. 66.

[8] Ellinwood, *Questions and Phases*, pp. 136–137.

[9] Dr. and Mrs. Howard Taylor, *Hudson Taylor's Spiritual Secrets*, Philadelphia, China Inland Mission, 1935, p. 23.

[10] Killion, *George Muller and the Quest*, pp. 7–8.

[11] Ellinwood, *Questions and Phases*, pp. 133–134.

[12] Klaus Fiedler, *The Story of Faith Missions: From Hudson Taylor to Present Day Africa*, Irvine, Regnum Books International 1994, pp. 11–25.

[13] Bliss, *A Concise History*, pp. 65–66.

[14] Edward Pfeiffer, *Mission Studies: Historical Survey and Outlines of Missionary Principles and Practice*, Columbus, Lutheran Book Concern, 1912, p. 72.

[15] Killion, *George Muller and the Quest*, p13.

[16] Taylor, *Hudson Taylor's Spiritual Secrets*, pp. 11–12.

[17] Dr. and Mrs. Howard Taylor, *Hudson Taylor and the China Inland Mission: The Growth of a Work of God*, London, China Inland Mission, 1955, p. 379.

[18] Bliss, *A Concise History*, p. 66.

[19] Ellinwood, *Questions and Phases*, pp. 141–142.

Miracles Do Happen

A missionary colleague, Ray, tells us about how God provided that new blue Volkswagen.

In the spring of 1965 I was asked to go to Seattle to take a temporary training assignment. Since the trip was 4,000 miles round trip, and I knew I would be asked to go in subsequent summers, I began to think seriously about purchasing a new car. My desire was for a Volkswagen as it seemed the most practical in terms of price, economy and reliability. Not having the funds, I decided to take some time off and work to earn the money.

During an across-the-border training program that year, while directing a phase of the training program, I had the opportunity to play host to a tour group from the States. The group came over for the day, and stayed the night. At the end of the day, a pastor and a business man came over to my *champa* (thatched hut) to chat. Eventually the conversation turned to discussing my plans for the next months.

I told them about the long journey to the training assignment and the need for a car. The pastor challenged me to pray about the need and not think about leaving to go to work. "In fact," said the pastor, "let's pray about the need right now. And we will continue to pray about your need for a car."

Several weeks passed when a letter came from the businessman who had sat around the campfire that night and who had joined the pastor and me in praying about the car. The businessman said in his letter, "The Lord has been nudging to buy a Volkswagen. I've been looking at some used ones."

While the letter was a real encouragement, and though I was afraid of offending, I wrote back and said "I'm really hoping for a NEW Volkswagen."

Weeks passed; we were closing down our training program but no word came. I thought the offer had probably fallen through.

One night, just before falling asleep, I prayed once again and told the Lord, "I really need a new car." Immediately, I sensed an assurance that A NEW CAR WAS MINE.

The very next day a letter came from the businessman saying, "There is a new 1965 Sea Blue V.W. with only fifty miles on it, parked in my driveway. It's yours when you come through here."

CHAPTER THREE

• • • • • • • • • •

Living By Faith Alone
The Test of Scripture

"It is not intolerant to reject falsehood, neither are we tolerant when we warmly appraise and accept [unsound] ideas. But in our wise intolerance we must not lose our love; and in our tolerance we must not give away our souls."—William Barclay

As you already know, I was hooked on the ideology of living by faith. As you know, too, I began studying the Bible, trying to find out what other faith missionaries knew that I didn't.

One day I decided to study every passage in the New Testament that contained the word *faith* or the word *believe*.

I didn't begin my scriptural search with the following questions. Remember, I really was looking for the doctrine of living by faith. These questions flowed from my research.

Does the Bible present a clear mandate for missionaries to go to assignments without the complete financial support of God's people, to go by faith alone?

Do the Scriptures teach that financial resources are always gained through the prayer of faith, with no other means, or methods employed? This is the rallying cry and ideology of the true faith missionary.[1]

Is there a special God-designed economy for faith missionaries that doesn't apply to any other Christian worker, like pastors, and others filling full-time positions for the church? Are faith missionaries exempt from all the teaching of Scripture—Old Testament and New Testament—regarding financial responsibilities, financial planning, and financial provision?

What does the Bible say?

It's especially important for faith missionaries to be sure of their scriptural ground. Yet many faith missionaries either do not know what biblical texts are used to support the live-by-faith system or knowing the popular texts, have never personally examined them. It's also true many faith missionaries refer to Carey, Müller, or Taylor and not to Scripture for support of the ideology.

It's important to put the ideology to the test, to the test of Scripture. In this chapter we will examine the biblical texts most often used by faith missionaries to justify going to their assignments without complete financial support. These texts have been and still are the foundation of many prayers for God's miraculous intervention, particularly for financial needs. There has been a strong commitment to this belief. [3]

The three biblical passages are Luke 9:1–6, the story of Jesus sending out the Twelve; Elijah's story recorded in 1 Kings 17 through 2 Kings 1, particularly the feeding by ravens; and Matthew 6:25–34 when Jesus challenged the disciples' faith.

In Luke 9:2–6 Jesus sent out his disciples in this manner, *Take nothing for the journey—no staff, no bag, no bread, no money, no extra tunic.*

In this clear-cut, simply stated phrase, *Take nothing for the journey,* Jesus seemed to be laying down a principle for all disciples. But was he?

It is not difficult to see how this text might be used to justify trusting in God alone, through faith and prayer, for financial provision. Will this application stand the test?

To find out, let's continue with Jesus to discover if He meant this as a principle for all time, for all missionaries. In Luke twenty–two, Jesus, perhaps anticipating the very issue we are examining, reminds the disciples of that earlier command, *Take nothing for the journey—no staff, no bag, no bread, no extra tunic.*

Changed conditions bring changed methods.

Luke 22:35–36, Jesus asked them, "When I sent you without purse, bag or sandals, did you lack anything?"

"Nothing," they answered.

He said to them, "But now if you have a purse, take it, and also a bag; and if you don't have a sword, sell your cloak and buy one."

But now. Here, at a time when Jesus Christ our Lord was sharing a last supper with the disciples and preparing for the cross, His last day on earth, Jesus sends a strong and perhaps unexpected signal.

Jesus clearly rescinds the original command and strongly indicates there will be a different way. Robertson, in *Word Pictures In The New Testament* sums it up like this: "Changed conditions bring changed needs."[5]

Now they need everything they can get their hands on.

Matthew Henry comments,

"He [Jesus] gives notice of a very great change of their circumstances now approaching."[6]

The *Interpreter's One-Volume Commentary* makes this observation, "Now they need everything they can get their hands on, even a sword."[7]

Obviously, Jesus uses overemphasis here (a sword?) so that the disciples will not miss the point. It's as if Jesus were saying "Don't miss this. Don't expect things to happen now like they did when I sent you out with nothing." The earlier instruction in Luke nine was a special case for that limited time and situation.

Elijah, fed by the ravens (1 Kings 17:2–6), is often used as a justifying text by those who accept the live-by-faith philosophy. In the twenty-eight times Elijah is referred to in the New Testament, not once is his experience cited in any context where financial provision is under discussion. The Elijah experience is never used by any other prophet or priest of the Old Testament to instruct Israel in how financial needs should be met. It was a special case for that time and situation. It is spurious and spiritually dangerous to make application of this story the way some faith missionaries have done.[8] The way I did.

The disciples' experience in Luke nine, and Elijah's experience were special cases.

The greatest error missionaries can make...

This may be the greatest error faith missionaries make in building a by-faith-alone ideology: observing a special case in the Scriptures then assuming it as, applying it as, the general case for their lives.

It has been said that when interpreting Scripture we must be careful to know the difference when a text is descriptive and when it is prescriptive. The descriptive/prescriptive principle of interpretation is especially appropriate when studying the experiences of a prophet like Elijah.

Missionaries (Christians in any walk of life) can experience special acts of God on their behalf, including receiving money. But to make a general principle out of a special case is unrealistic and unjustified.

It is necessary to reach way back to the seventeenth century to discover the roots of the live-by-faith ideology. The ideology originated with a movement called pietism. "It [pietism] stressed emotion, the commitment of the will, and [an experience of] conversion...."[9] The three original independent faith missions "had their origin in pietism...."[10]

The movement began with Philip Jacob Spener (1635–1705).

"Spener was intent upon a moral and spiritual reformation.

He was grieved by controversy over doctrine, sometimes bitter as it was and often arid and having little direct bearing upon everyday living. Much of the contemporary preaching was of that kind. The lives of many of the clergy were unworthy and among the laity, partly as an aftermath of the long war [thirty-years war] there were drunkenness and immorality. Church services tended to be formal and sterile. What he stressed was genuine conversion and the cultivation of the Christian life. To this end he discounted doctrinal sermons, preached the necessity of the new birth, a personal, warm, Christian experience, and the cultivation of Christian virtues."[11]

Bernhard Ramm, in his book *Protestant Biblical Interpretation*, while reviewing different schools of interpretation, stated that the pietistic movement embraced a method which he called "devotional interpretation."

Ramm pointed out *two weaknesses* in the method.

One, "It falls prey to allegorization especially in the use of the Old Testament. In the effort to find a spiritual truth or application of a passage of Scripture the literal and therefore primary meaning of the passage is obscured. If it is not a case of bald allegorizing it may be excessive typology. Given enough allegorical and typological rope one may prove a variety of contradictory propositions from the Old Testament."

Given enough allegorical and typological rope, one may prove a variety of contradictory propositions from the Old Testament.

Two, "Devotional interpretation may be a substitute for the requisite exegetical and doctrinal studies of the Bible."[12]

Even though doctrine was seemingly not a strength, pietists had many other strengths, and one was their commitment to missions. Some of the earliest missionaries mentioned in the history of seventeenth and eighteenth centuries' Christianity were sent out from August Hermann Franke's ministry at the University of Halle in Germany. Franke was one of the first pietists, a disciple of Philip Jacob Spener.

Ramm's observations about pietists are particularly interesting because Müller was deeply influenced by pietists. Müller became a Christian while under the influence of August Hermann Franke. Fiedler observed that Hudson Taylor's guiding theological principle was not dogmatic correctness but effective evangelism.[13] There was a strong link from the pietists to Müller to Taylor.

Regarding Müller and the influence of pietism, it was Franke who began an orphanage ministry and was the originator of the idea of telling no one about the financial needs of the orphanage: just pray. Müller was not only saved under Franke's ministry, but was greatly influenced by Franke's conviction that the needs of his orphanage were met only as a result of prayer. Müller went to England as a missionary to the Jews under the influence of Franke. It was in England that Müller, after some years of struggle, eventually chose orphanages as a ministry. He began propagating the idea of prayer and faith as the only means of financing the ministry, and eventually had a strong influence on Hudson Taylor.

Christians (missionaries) brought up within this ideological framework (believing prayer is the method through which financial needs are met), beginning with the influence of Franke and Müller, and those who wrote about them, continuing on through the twentieth century, tended to interpret certain passages of Scripture to support the ideology. The Elijah story is one of those passages.

In reality, Elijah had nothing to do with the act of provision at the Kerith Ravine: *"You will drink from the brook, and I have ordered the ravens to feed you there"* (1 Kings 17:4). When this text is used to support the notion that one just prays and God provides, it is being misinterpreted and misapplied. Elijah was under specific orders, and so were the ravens. Elijah's prayers are not mentioned as a factor. And yet, Elijah's story is often cited in missionary circles as the ground for prayer and trust in

God alone as the means of provision: miraculous provision. To what extent Franke, Müller, or Taylor authorized or encouraged the use of this text as a basis of such a belief is not certain. But that it became a cornerstone of the ideology, is without question.

Elijah had another experience which some people use as a proof text to support the ideology. In 1 Kings 17:13–16 we read that Elijah told the widow the jar of flour and jug of oil would not be used up for many days, and it wasn't. Anyone who uses the Raven or the Widow texts as proof of the ideology needs to be prepared to be able to raise, by faith, someone from the dead. Elijah did that, too. (1 Kings 17:22; *The Lord heard Elijah's cry, and the boy's life returned to him, and he lived.*)

Any missionary who has received direct instructions from God as Elijah did, with the means of provision specified (in Elijah's case ravens; jar of flour and jug of oil) should not hesitate to respond, and go. However, without a special revelation such as Elijah's, it would be nothing but presumption.

Unity of Scripture (the internal harmony of Scripture) is a primary principle of biblical interpretation. To use Elijah's experiences as the basis of provision for all missionaries violates the principle of unity. In a later chapter you'll see that Elijah's experiences with God's provision did not reflect the general principles specifically taught throughout the Old and New Testaments regarding financial provision. It was a special case.

> "Unity and harmony of Scripture is a primary principle of biblical interpretation."

A third text, perhaps the most-often cited by the proponents of living by faith, is Matthew 6:28–34.

"And why do you worry about clothes? See how the lilies of the field grow. They do not labor or spin. Yet I tell you that not even Solomon in all his splendor was dressed like one of these. If that is how God clothes the grass of the field, which is here today and tomorrow is thrown into the fire, will he not much more clothe you, O you of little faith? So do not worry, saying, 'What shall we eat?' or 'What

shall we wear?' For the pagans run after all these things, and your heavenly Father knows that you need them. But seek first his kingdom and his righteousness, and all these things will be given to you as well. Therefore do not worry about tomorrow, for tomorrow will worry about itself. Each day has enough trouble of its own."

Why do you worry?

First of all this text isn't about money, or provision. It is about *worry*. It begins with worry: *And why do you worry about clothes?* Worry is mentioned again right in the middle of the passage, *So do not worry*. And, it ends with worry: *Therefore do not worry about tomorrow for tomorrow will worry about itself.*

So do not worry.

So, what did the Lord mean with the admonition *"O you of little faith."* Some have concluded from this that the necessities of life are dependent entirely upon an application of one's faith, through prayer. How do they arrive at that conclusion?

Do not worry.

The statements, *Your heavenly Father knows you have need of them,"* and *"Seek first his kingdom and his righteousness, and all these things will be given to you as well* seem to imply that all thought of material things should be abandoned; just trust the Lord in faith and seek his kingdom and one's needs will be supplied, if you pray. Is that really what he meant?

It is easy to see, particularly if the reader approaches this text with a preconceived notion of what the text teaches, how a living-by-faith doctrine could be implied. However, reading the text in the Amplified New Testament throws light upon its real meaning, and helps us to understand the application. In verse thirty-three Jesus himself helps us make the correct application.

Please note that the Amplified New Testament editorial committee used parenthesis to "signify additional phases of meaning included in the Greek word, phrase or clause," and brackets "contain justified clarifying words or comments not actually expressed in the immediate Greek text."

"But seek for (aim at and strive after) first of all His kingdom, and His righteousness [His way of doing and being right], and

then all these things taken together will be given you besides."

We are to *"aim at and strive after His way of doing and being right."* This is precisely what it *does* mean to live by faith: find out His way of doing and being right in whatever arena of life we are engaged in. Then, we are seeking the kingdom, and living by the principles of the kingdom. Then, *"all these things will be given you...."*

In some well-known commentaries we read how this major misapplication of Matthew 6:28–34 is addressed. It seems as if each commentator was aware of the problem of misapplication, and wanted to make sure the reader didn't get the wrong interpretation/application.

For example, Jamison, Faucett, and Brown comment, "Thought or forethought, for temporal things—in the sense of reflection, consideration—is required alike by Scripture and common sense. It is that anxious solicitude, that carking [anxious, troublesome, oppressive, annoying] care, which springs from unbelieving doubts and misgivings, which alone is here condemned. The argument here [the illustration from the "fowls"] is from the greater to the less.... The brute creation—void of reason—are incapable of sowing, reaping, and storing; yet your heavenly Father suffers them not helplessly to perish, but sustains them without any of the processes: will He see, then, His own children using all the means which reason dictates for procuring the things needful for the body—looking up to Himself at every step—and yet leave them to starve? Let it never be forgotten that what our Lord here condemns is not attention to business, nor any amount or range of thought on the subject of it which may be necessary for its most successful prosecution...."[14]

Matthew Henry comments:

"As to present sustenance, we may and must use lawful means to get it, else we tempt God; we must be diligent in our callings,

"Aim at and strive after his way of doing and being right...."

"This is precisely what it means to live by faith."

and prudent in proportioning our expenses to what we have, and we must pray for daily bread; and if all other means fail, we may and must ask relief of those that are able to give it."

And, "This does not forbid a prudent foresight, and preparation accordingly, but a perplexing solicitude, and a prepossession of difficulties and calamities, which may perhaps never come, or if they do, may be easily borne, and the evil of them guarded against."[15]

George Müller comments, "When I first began to allow God to deal with me, relying on Him, taking Him at His Word, and set out fifty years ago simply relying on Him for myself, family, taxes, travelling expenses and every other need, I rested on the simple promises I found in the sixth chapter of Matthew...."[16]

How did Müller conclude from this passage in Matthew chapter six there was a promise that if he only prayed, and told no one else but God of his needs, God would always provide?

As Ellinwood observed when reviewing the history of the doctrine of living by faith, "Prayer without the use of means, where means can be employed, is a new doctrine."[17]

"Prayer without the use of means, where means can be employed, is a new doctrine."

It is not just a "new doctrine" but an extra-biblical doctrine: an ideology.

Müller, himself, when commenting during an interview, makes this interesting statement about the philosophy of living by faith:

"Do not, however, expect to obtain full faith at once. All such things as jumping into full exercise of faith in such things, I discountenance. I do not believe in it. *I do not believe in it, I do **NOT** believe in it and wish you plainly to understand I do not believe in it.*"[18]

The italics, capitalization, and bolding in the above quote are the original author's.

"The ground of faith is correct interpretation."

It is interesting to realize Müller made the above exclamatory comment near the close of his life: 1898. This is also about the time when some of the unfortunate experiences cited in this book were taking place. Could it be that Müller was beginning to hear of how the live-by-faith philosophy was being erroneously applied, was not happy with what he was hearing, and was making a belated attempt to put some distance between himself and the "new doctrine?"

Barclay comments on Matthew six: "It is not ordinary, prudent foresight, such as becomes a man, that Jesus forbids; it is worry. Jesus is not advocating a shiftless, thriftless, reckless, thoughtless, improvident attitude to life; he is forbidding a care-worn, worried fear...."[19]

What is, therefore, His way of doing and being right in the arena of raising and maintaining support? Living by faith, to borrow the phrase, is living by the principles of the kingdom: the principles of righteousness. Knowing the principles of the kingdom and striving to live by them is the standing order; this is truly living by faith.

As the theologians have told us for a long time, there is a ground of faith. Ground implies something solid, basic. Correct interpretation and application of the Bible is the solid and sure ground of faith.

Jesus was not saying in Matthew six we should abandon all other principles about financial provision, and abandon ourselves to God, and that God would, then, because of our faith and prayers alone, supply our needs in miraculous and mysterious ways.

Jesus was saying know the principles of the kingdom, live by them, and you will not have to worry about the necessities of life. This is living by faith.

There is a system of provision underlying the Matthew six text, but it is not a system based upon one's individual faith.

Just as for the lilies, God has provided a system, a plan

"In every one of those places where our interpretation is at fault, we have made substitution of the voice of man for the voice of God."[20]

• 47 • • • • • • • •

for meeting the needs of those who walk with Him, or those whom He leads into Christian service. This is how one lives by faith—by the system—by God's plan, by the rules of the kingdom—by the biblical principles governing any domain of life, we might be concerned about. Our special concern, of course, is the support of full-time Christian workers called missionaries.

The principles are the same whether serving as a pastor, minister of music, doctor, truck driver or missionary.

Actually, the principles are the same whether serving as a pastor, minister of music, doctor, truck driver, or missionary. *"The laborer is worthy of his hire"* (Luke 10:7) is the universal principle upon which all remuneration is based.

There is no special system, with separate rules, for the missionary. That's part of the myth.

There are not two separate and distinct economies taught in Scripture. Missionaries are not exempt from the profound and pervasive principles taught in Scripture regarding financial well-being. These principles are summed up in the statement: "The laborer is worthy of his hire." It is not faith-generated prayer that is "worthy," but one's "labor."

It was the labor—the ministry of helping orphans and taking the Gospel to China—that the people of Müller's and Taylor's days were responding to. And the record is clear, people didn't respond until they were told.

By saying these things, the intent is not to throw out prayer as an influence or factor in raising support. Missionaries should, among other things, focus their prayers on seeking God's help to:

1. Be the kind of person (quality of Christian life) people will want to support.
2. Be doing the kinds of things in ministry and service that will demonstrate they are a worthy laborer right now.
3. Be active in raising support and bathe these activities in prayer.
4. Seek doors of opportunity to share their ministry.

5. Enlist the help of Christian friends and family.

Basing our lives upon wrong concepts (myths) can have disturbing results. Missionaries who have gone out by faith and for whom this system of living by faith has not worked can come to disturbing conclusions and unhappy experiences.

Some missionaries who struggle with finances question God about it. They might have the attitude that God is obligated to provide for them because they are going without daily necessities. They might think their willingness to go without makes God obligated to supply their needs. After all, look what they gave up to serve God. God owes them.

They didn't start out with the God-owes-me attitude. It surfaced when the money didn't come and the pressure mounted. Some missionaries might even hold their mission agency responsible if their personal monetary needs are not being met.

When God is held solely responsible for the lack of money by faith missionaries, these same missionaries will themselves usually do nothing to solve the problem. They went out; totally depending upon God. Therefore, the problem is God's to solve. They might even feel it would be morally and spiritually wrong to personally do anything about it—like write to their friends and partners to tell them what is happening. To tell anyone but God would be a violation of their spiritual/ethical commitment to the myth—the ideology.

Not only is God obligated to provide because the missionary left all and went out to the mission field with nothing, but sometimes dissatisfaction is expressed this way:

"Why isn't He providing when I work so hard? I'm suffering from the climate and diseases, leaving my family for days at a time. Why isn't He doing what He said—that if I would seek first His kingdom—He would provide? What's wrong with God?"

"When [correct interpretation] is absent not only have [we] misinterpreted the Word, but [we] have taken [extracted] falsehood out of the truth."[21]

Or, in an extremity, *"What's wrong with me?"* This may be the most difficult question a missionary asks, and then he struggles for an answer.

"Is my faith not strong enough? Have I done something wrong? Is there some sin in my life that is holding God back?"

"If a missionary's wage is based upon his lack of sin, what hope is there for any missionary?"

If a missionary's wage is based upon lack of sin, what hope is there for any missionary?

"If you are really spiritual you will be satisfied with whatever comes in. You will be satisfied to suffer without sufficient finances."

That attitude is often heard in faith mission circles. It cannot be said that Christian workers will never suffer—even suffer financially—but how does the suffering servant mentality stack up against Jesus' own statement,

"The laborer is worthy of his hire."

Should a missionary plan for poverty?

Should the missionary base spiritual life, warfare, and welfare upon a foundation of financial weakness?

Some faith missions have had an interesting history of adjustment to the realities of their missionaries' financial challenges. In the early years of the modern missionary movement, many missionaries went to their assignments without a complete partnership team. Many new missionaries responded to the challenge "Just come, God will provide." Some went with as little as 50% of budget, and some with less. In time, however, these missions had to change their policies to require some fixed level of pledged support. Why? Because the former system wasn't working for many of their missionaries. God was not providing. Some missionaries incurred "red accounts." A red account meant the missionary was in debt to the mission agency. The organization could not carry the accumulative effects of these debts.

In some missions, subsequent organizational experience shows that an even higher level of pledged support was needed.

One-hundred percent of pledged support is more and more becoming the norm.

During these years of transition and adjustment, these faith-agencies developed supplemental funds from which low-on-support missionaries could draw. Like red accounts, though, this proved to be a kind of "black hole" for the organizations. Parameters were adopted that limited the use of such supplemental funds.

Interestingly, and ironically, some faith missionaries considered the supplemental fund as God's response to their faith. They were disturbed when such sources of income were taken away. These missionaries believed living off these funds was living by faith, the fund was God's provision.

Other missionaries would not accept anything from such a fund because it would, in their minds, violate the principle of trusting God only.

We see, then, even within the circle of the proponents of living by faith, exactly opposite applications from people who claim they believe the same fundamental truth.

Paying the bills every month is a reality every missionary lives with, just as it is a reality for the missionary's financial partners. Reality has a way of pushing back the fog of myth for all of us.

If we look into Scripture, past the popular interpretation/application of certain texts we've looked at in this chapter (part of the fog), we will find a beautiful plan presented to us. It is a plan based upon centuries-old principles.

The Holy Spirit used the apostle Paul, through his sometimes discouraging personal experience with financial support, and his inspired teaching, to instruct us well in these principles.

There is wonderful unity in the Word of God. Every principle taught in the New Testament relating to the material support of a Christian worker has its roots in the Old Testament.

"There should be great freedom of personal belief and great charity for those who differ from us, but a dangerous responsibility lies in the inculcation of a belief among others which may involve them in fatal danger and lead them in turn to disseminate among still others, views which cannot be supported either by scriptural authority, or by the experience of the Christian church."[22]

The patterns are clear. The principles enduring.
Let's continue to listen for the *ring of truth*.

END NOTES

[1] Frank F. Ellinwood, *Questions and Phases of Modern Missions*, Dodd, Mead and Company, 1899, p. 133. As Ellinwood points out, the whole theological/missiological issue centers on the concept of "means." Faith missions determined to reject certain methods of gaining financial support: certain means. Fundamentally, what was rejected was asking: asking directly for financial support. When Ellinwood wrote in 1899, he stated that faith missions didn't expect "a greater divine blessing" because they rejected asking directly for money. I disagree with that conclusion. Many faith missionaries did come to expect greater blessing, and looked down upon mission agencies that wrote and spoke directly of their financial needs. This is true today, in some circles.

[2] Bernard Ramm, *Protestant Biblical Interpretation, A Textbook of Hermeneutics for Conservative Protestants*, Boston, W.A. Wilde Company, 1956, p. 1.

[3] J.H. Hunter, *Flame of Fire*, The Sudan Interior Mission, 1961, p. 235. That living by faith is an ideology with strong emotional commitment can be clearly seen as Hunter writes: "We are well aware that to many people, even professing Christians, this faith principle is incomprehensible. They find it too intangible a thing to venture one's life upon. To them it is fantastic and inconsistent with 20th century realism that demands a more concrete foundation for a missionary enterprise than the abstract principles laid down by Christ and His followers 2,000 years ago. They forget that it has worked, is working and will continue to work till the moon is old and the stars are cold, and the books of the Judgment Day unfold."

[4] Ellinwood, Questions and Phases of Modern Missions, pp. 141–42.

[5] Archibald Thomas Robertson, *Word Pictures in the New Testament, The Gospel According To Luke,* Grand Rapids, Baker Book House, 1930, Volume II, p. 271.

[6] *Matthew Henry's Commentary on the Whole Bible, In Six Volumes, Matthew to John,* McLean, Virginia, MacDonald Publishing Company, Volume V, pp. 81–86.

[7] *The Interpreter's One-Volume Commentary,* Ed. by Charles M. Laymon, Nashville, Abingdon Press, 1984, p. 702. Jesus implies with the use of exaggeration that many methods (financial methods included) would be used in getting the Gospel to the ends of the earth. This is a startling contrast to the idea adopted by faith missions that they would dispense with certain means. By what authority?

[8] Ellinwood, *Questions and Phases of Modern Missions,* p. 135. Ellinwood is cited several times because he is the only author that I could find who, at that time in the history of missions, seriously questioned the ideology, an ideology that had begun to bear damaged fruit. For example, Ellinwood reports on nine missionaries who left the United States for Sierra Leone. Of the nine missionaries, three died. Two of these were strong believers in a "faith cure," and would take no medicine. "Two days later a third died of exhaustion from neglected fever, having been ill about nine days. As the fourth patient in the list refused the services of a physician, the latter reported to the Governor that the missionaries, by the course pursued, had developed a malignant type of fever, which endangered the whole community." Ellinwood concludes that these missionaries, "to all appearances died from insufficient support, and from a persistent reliance on faith instead of medicine in extreme sickness." Dispensing with certain means had another unfortunate consequence. The Governor quarantined the house the missionaries lived in and advised the survivors be sent back to America.

[9] Kenneth Scott Latourette, *A History Of Christianity,* New York, Harper and Brothers Publishers, 1953, p. 731.

[10] Klaus Fiedler, *The Story Of Faith Missions: From Hudson Taylor To Present Day Africa*, Irvine, California, Regnum Books International, 1994, pp. 20–25. Fiedler's book provides a very important historical background to what is called faith missions. He also notes the connection of faith missions to pietism and puritanism. The three original faith missions [at that time also called "independent missions"] had their "origin in pietism/puritanism." "Independent missions accepted no human authority beyond their own and were responsible to no church or missions...financial support came from what they earned, possibly from a secular job or as traders; sometimes they were people of independent means, and often they received support from friends at home.... Independent missions served as an example for faith missions insofar as, for them too, God's individual call was the starting point of their missiology.... Faith missions absorbed their basic ideas from the independent missions (the concept of direct and individual responsibility to God) and from the non–church missions (the concept of 'faith support'). When Hudson Taylor became an independent missionary, he took the decision to expect his support only 'as an answer to prayer in faith.'"

[11] Latourette, *A History of Christianity*, p. 895.

[12] Ramm, *Protestant Biblical Interpretation*, pp. 62–63. Ramm also says, p. 30, "The curse of the allegorical method is that it obscures the true meaning of the Word of God and had it not kept the Gospel truth central it would have become cultic and heretical," and, p. 31, "The allegorical method puts a premium on the subjective and the doleful result is the obscuration of the Word of God." Ramm quotes Fullerton, p. 31, "When the historical sense of a passage is once abandoned there is wanting any sound regulative principle to govern exegesis.... The mystical [allegorical] method of exegesis, is an unscientific and arbitrary method, reduces the Bible to obscure enigmas, undermines the authority of all interpretation, and therefore, when taken by itself, failed to meet the apologetic necessities of the time.'"

[13] Fiedler, *The Story Of Faith Missions*, p. 34.

[14] Jamieson, Fausset, and Brown, *A Commentary: Critical, Experimental and Practical: On the Old and New Testaments,* Matthew–John, Grand Rapids, William B. Erdmans Publishing Company, 1948 Volume V.

[15] *Matthew Henry's Commentary On The Whole Bible, Matthew to John,* McLean, Virginia, MacDonal Publishing Company, Volume V, pp. 81–86.

[16] A. Sims, ed., *George Müller Man of Faith,* Grand Rapids, Zondervan Publishing House, p.33.

[17] Ellinwood, *Questions and Phases Of Modern Missions,* p. 146.

[18] A. Sims, ed., *George Müller Man of Faith,* pp. 36–37.

[19] William Barclay, *The Gospel of Matthew,* The Daily Study Bible Series, Chapters 1–10, Revised Edition, Philadelphia, The Westminster Press, 1975, Volume I, p. 255.

[20] Ramm, *Protestant Biblical Interpretation,* p. 2.

[21] Ramm, *Protestant Biblical Interpretation,* p. xiii.

[22] Ellinwood, *Questions and Phases Of Modern Missions,* p. 144.

CHAPTER FOUR

The Triumph of Scripture

Biblical Precedents, Patterns, and Principles

In 1899, Royal and Eva Dye—missionaries with the Christian Church—went to Africa, supported by their denomination. The coastal steamer, Lagos with the Dyes aboard, visited several ports along the west coast. At each port, the captain's curious behavior caught the attention of his passengers.

This account describes one such incident.

At many of these stops the captain disembarked, carrying oddly shaped bundles. There was something furtive about these excursions of his, and he never spoke of them. Gossip ran high among the passengers as to what kind of contraband he might be carrying, or what nefarious trade he could be engaged in.

One night Royal, doing his evening turn about the ship, came upon the captain standing alone beside the rail. "Good evening," he said and started on. To his surprise, the captain motioned him to stop.

"How long before you'll be goin' back home?"

"How long before you'll be goin' back home?"

Royal, pleased at his interest, answered courteously, "About three years, sir. Our term of service calls for three years in the field, then one year's furlough."

"When you get home, lad, stay there." The man's voice was angry. "This comin' out to heathen lands and starvin' to death is plain foolish."

"We won't starve, sir. My salary isn't large, but we'll be taken care of."

"Hum! Guess that's what these folks thought, too, but now look at them!"

Since there were obviously no "other folks" to look at just then, Royal waited for the captain to continue.

When he spoke again he was still angry. "Whole families of 'em, missionaries, left stranded. Nobody lookin' out for 'em, no way to get home. What kind of business is that, I ask?" His eye fell on a poorly wrapped package lying on the deck.

Royal guessed the secret. The captain was likely sharing provisions with the stranded families. He proceeded cautiously. "Are there many of them, sir?"

"Not so many any more. Lots of 'em died. Some have beat their way home, hoppin' from one boat to another for a free ride! That's how I found out about them. But there's still plenty of 'em in here" — he pointed toward the interior, "How come nobody looks after 'em?" he asked belligerently.

"I guess they came out on faith, sir."[2]

"The intervention of broad oceans does not change the general laws of Christian service nor invalidate anywhere the divinely authorized principles that 'the laborer is worthy of his hire.' A guaranteed support is even more indispensable on the foreign field than at home. If one is to carry economy to the verge of starvation anywhere in Christ's service, a savage community in a malarious country is the very last place for the experiment."[1]

How many missionaries, over the years, have died unnecessarily, or were placed in desperate straights through lack of financial provision, and spiritual support of the folks at home? This answer will never be known.

I do know beliefs about finances have consequences. If the belief system is built upon inadequate, or incorrect doctrine, the consequences could be dramatic. It is not just *One Man's Story.* Just as in 1899, there are missionaries around the world, right now, as this book is being written, who are experiencing unwarranted and unnecessary hardness.

BELIEFS → ATTITUDES → ACTIONS

The missionaries in Royal Dye's account, who "came out on faith," had a belief system, a belief system similar to the belief system described in *One Man's Story*. Belief systems produce attitudes.

Bad beliefs produce bad attitudes and self-defeating actions; good beliefs produce good attitudes, and productive actions.

Attitudes do have a source, and they do have consequences. This formula helps us see the connection:

Belief System → Attitudes → Actions[3]

The relationship of attitudes back to beliefs and forward to actions has been thoroughly studied in the realm of psychology. Most researchers begin with the concept attitude, and explore the relationship of attitude to other human dynamics often described in the research as actions. The exact words "belief" and "actions" are not always used by the researchers. However, these concepts are consistently present in their discussions even though other words may be used.[4]

"Beliefs and attitudes are the basis of action, or lack of action."

Beliefs and attitudes are the basis of action—destructive, productive—or, in too many missionaries' lives, no action. It's sometimes hard to sort these elements out in real life, but very often they can be traced if we, with God's help, take the time.

When inappropriate attitudes (referring back to the story in chapter one) like irresponsibility, passivity, sloth, etc. show up, the natural question to ask is, "Why?" Where do attitudes like these come from? What would cause a normally responsible person to be irresponsible?

Let's go back to the space ship illustration to help uncover the answer. Space travel that is safe, resulting in "mission accomplished," requires reliable reference points. The space ship's guidance system may use Earth, another planet, and a distant star for its points of reference. Shifting of a reference point, or an absent reference point, or a faulty guidance system would mean disaster.

The internal guidance system, monitoring the reference points, sets the attitude of the space ship. Correct or incorrect attitude determines success, or failure of the mission.

Using space travel as an analogy—imagining the space ship as a missionary—and changing the reference points to the Bible, to missionaries' experiences, and to traditions of the faith missionary enterprise, the relationship of reference points to a missionary's attitudes can be visualized.

If the reference points (Bible, experience, and traditions) are thought of as the source of beliefs about raising support and these reference points determine attitudes, and if one of the reference points is missing, or the data coming from that reference point is flawed, then the missionary's personal, internal guidance system will produce faulty attitudes. The missionary's actions will be inappropriate or nonexistent and he will miss the target: the target of having a complete partnership team.

Going back to the attitudes talked about in *One Man's Story*, I didn't realize in the belief system I had constructed, the biblical reference point was almost nonexistent.

I bought so deeply into the idea of living by faith from books and stories (reference points of experience and tradition) of and about faith missionaries I didn't realize my belief system was built upon the invalid, inadequate reference points of tradition and experience. Not totally invalid but without the Word of God to act as overseer, tradition and experience can take an unrealistic and dominant place, overshadowing and even excluding the Word of God.

No wonder attitudes can be so self-destructive. When I asked myself the question, "Why have I been so irresponsible about financial support?" I was led right back to my belief: *It's because it was God's responsibility to provide, not mine.* Unfortunately, that belief of God being responsible didn't come from the Bible.

When I asked myself the question, "Why didn't I do something [take action] about our lack of support?" It led me right back to the belief that those who live by the ideology of faith alone don't do anything but pray.

With the Bible missing as a reference point, is it any wonder there were faulty attitudes? Any wonder at the lack of support?

The Bible is **the** key reference point for a belief system about support raising. The teachings of the Bible must be present and dominant within any missionary's belief system about this subject. One's attitudes depend upon it. Success depends upon it.

The Bible is the **star of the show.** A star illumines all of the other heavenly bodies found in its orbit. Just like a star, the Bible provides the spiritual illumination and consequent guidance every Christian needs. The Bible lights up the terrain (traditions and experiences) upon which the Christian travels. The Bible excels and performs brilliantly in its role. *Your Word is a lamp to my feet and a light to my path* (Psalm 119:105).

SELF SUPPORT: THE APOSTLE PAUL

The apostle Paul and Barnabas, are arguably the church's first selected and appointed missionaries. There is a valid belief system about support from Paul's experience and teaching and it is recorded for us in Scripture.

It's interesting how the Holy Spirit led this great apostle down a trail marked with some discouragement and frustration about the issue of support, and ultimately to some answers for himself, answers for all of us.

Let's go down the trail with him and find out what he did, what frustrated him, and what the Holy Spirit led him to teach.

By examining the apostle's life and teaching, and the circumstantial flow of events, a composite emerges. The composite explained in the following pages represents reliable understanding of God's plan for how the support of full-time Christian workers is to be provided.

The apostle's experience as a commissioned, sent-out missionary began in Acts, chapter thirteen.

"In the church at Antioch there were prophets and teachers: Barnabas, Simeon called Niger, Lucius of Cyrene, Manaen (who had been brought up with Herod the tetrarch) and Saul. While they were worshiping the Lord and fasting, the Holy Spirit said, 'Set apart for me Barnabas and Saul for the work to which I have called them.' So after they had fasted and prayed, they placed their hands on them and sent them off. The two of them sent on their way by the Holy Spirit went down to Seleucia and sailed from there to Cyprus" (Acts 13:1–4).

"Set apart for me Barnabas and Saul for the work to which I have called them."

When Paul and Barnabas were sent by the church at Antioch, it was without financial support. This is a legitimate conclusion because we find Paul working as a tent maker. Neither Paul or the young church knew how support of a full-time Christian worker was supposed to function. Self-support seemed to be the assumed strategy. Based upon what we, today, see in the New Testament Scriptures—something the young church did not have—it seems justifiable to conclude the church at Antioch should have supported at least Barnabas and Paul (John Mark was apparently not selected and affirmed by the leadership at Antioch).

The church was finding its way in a spiritual life that was new and dynamic. The church at Antioch was made up of members who were not necessarily steeped in, or even familiar with Old Testament principles regarding the Temple worker. The church at Antioch was cosmopolitan in ethnic makeup with members from Roman, Greek, and Hebrew backgrounds, to

"Why didn't the Holy Spirit instruct the prophets and teachers at Antioch to see to it that the church at Antioch financed Paul and Barnabas?"

name only the dominant groups. Paul, himself, was new at this business of being a sent-out missionary. He did not, apparently, think anything was out of order. But as we see from his later, high-on-the-learning-curve experience and teaching, Paul concluded the principles from the Old Testament were still true and should be applied to the New Testament church and its workers. His conclusions are what we find in his appeal to the Corinthians, in chapter nine of first Corinthians, which we will come to later. However in the first days of being missionaries, as they leave Antioch it is with the intention to support themselves, or if not the intention, it was soon a necessity.

Why didn't the Holy Spirit instruct the prophets and teachers at Antioch to see to it that the church at Antioch financed Paul and Barnabas?

WHY SELF-SUPPORT?

There were at least three reasons: because of a strategy of ministry, the cultural circumstances of the time, and the young church at Antioch wasn't ready for it. This third reason can't be documented; it's an assumption. First, the strategy of ministry.

"After this, Paul left Athens and went to Corinth. There he met a Jew named Aquila, a native of Pontus, who had recently come from Italy with his wife Priscilla, because Claudius had ordered all the Jews to leave Rome. Paul went to see them, and because he was a tentmaker as they were, he stayed and worked with them. Every Sabbath he reasoned in the synagogue, trying to persuade Jews and Greeks" (Acts 18:1–4).

Because Paul's missionary team initially took the Gospel to the synagogue, which met on Saturdays, Paul had some other days of the week to work at his trade. The plain facts of the situation allowed time for work. It wasn't a question of rightness or wrongness in terms of missionary strategy.

There were other reasons why Paul worked. He said this to

the Ephesian elders: *"I have not coveted anyone's silver or gold or clothing. You yourselves know that these hands of mine have supplied my own needs and the needs of my companions. In everything I did, I showed you that by this kind of hard work we must help the weak, remembering the words the Lord Jesus himself said: 'It is more blessed to give than to receive'"* (Acts 20:33–35).

"In everything I did I showed you."

Apparently, in the culture of that day, and among Christians of that culture, there were some who were not doing an "honest day's work." Paul says, *"In everything I did, I showed you...."* He was, as other translators render it, an example; a model. He himself needed to be a giver. He needed to help the weak. His work even supplied the needs of his fellow missionaries. Of course, we could say the reason was that he simply needed the money, but as we see there were far deeper issues, one of which was to be a model worker. Earning his keep.

Each of us, if we are missionaries, need to examine ourselves and make sure we are modeling the behavior we expect from others—from others who might support us.

One missionary candidate tells how when he reached 40% of the amount of money his organization required he "hit the wall." He just couldn't get beyond that level of support. As he was mulling this over, it came to him that he hadn't been giving a tithe—a tithe he had promised. When the tithe was resumed, and caught up, a dramatic increase in support followed. It wasn't long before he had full support.

THE BEGINNINGS OF PARTNERSHIP: A DIFFERENT SUPPORT STRATEGY

"When Silas and Timothy came from Macedonia, Paul devoted himself exclusively to preaching, testifying to the Jews that Jesus was the Christ" (Acts 18:5).

The strategy changed when Silas and Timothy came from Macedonia: *Paul devoted himself exclusively to preaching....* Paul was "set free from tent-making for a while so that he began to devote himself...with fresh consecration to preaching."[6]

We know from other passages that money came to Paul from the Macedonian churches more than once. When money was available the strategy changed. It was a practical thing, not a missiological issue.

The Macedonian church, by sending Silas and Timothy with money, points out the fact that another principle was beginning to surface in the life of Paul the missionary. He was beginning to receive support. He speaks of it directly, and by inference, to the church at Rome and to the church at Corinth.

"I hope to visit you while passing through and to have you assist me on my journey there [to Spain] ..." (Romans 15:24).

"Perhaps I will stay with you awhile, or even spend the winter, so that you can help me on my journey, wherever I go" (1 Corinthians 16:6).

"And when I was with you and needed something, I was not a burden to anyone, for the brothers who came from Macedonia supplied what I needed. I have kept myself from being a burden to you in any way, and will continue to do so" (2 Corinthians 11:9).

Paul is experiencing partnership, while he continued to work, when necessary. Partnership in ministry begins to surface as the practical means through which a full-time ministry could be carried out. There comes a time when he feels compelled to teach the principles of partnership to the church at Corinth.

Great lessons can be learned as we read these clearly spelled-out principles of why and how a Christian worker should be supported.

PARTNERS IN MINISTRY: THE TEACHING

The following passage, 1 Corinthians 9:1–9, is quoted from the Phillips, a paragraph at a time with a few comments of in-

"This chief apostle [Paul] or missionary, whose constant prayers for the success of his mission work, and for the constancy and growth of his converts are mentioned in nearly every epistle, never created emergencies and then prayed God to help him out without other effort." [5]

terpretation and application. It is possible the Holy Spirit had Paul write this chapter just for Christian workers, and for the people of God who provide the support. We all need to know how it should work.

Chapter nine of 1 Corinthians is a kind of Magna Carta based upon the apostle's own arguments to the Corinthians of why they should be supporting him and Barnabas. Chapter nine is also the biblical centerpiece of the composite I am building. There is no other passage in the New Testament where the subject of support for full-time workers is discussed so completely.

A Portfolio of Spiritual Work (Verses 1–3)

"Is there any doubt that I am a genuine messenger, any doubt that I am a free man? Have I not seen Jesus our Lord with my own eyes? Are not you yourselves samples of my work for the Lord? Even if other people should refuse to recognize my divine commission, yet to you at any rate I shall always be a true messenger, for you are a living proof of God's call to me. This is my real ground of defense to those who cross-examine me."

Every full-time missionary and missionary candidate must have a portfolio of service. The apostle just presented his *PORTFOLIO* of ministry and service to the Corinthians. Every full-time Christian worker must ask:

Am I a *genuine messenger?* How has God validated my being a missionary?

Have I *seen Jesus?* Is my testimony clear and persuasive?

Are there *samples of my work?* Do I have a portfolio of service and ministry that demonstrates my value to interested persons or churches? Have I earned the right to be selected and sent and supported?

Are not you yourselves samples of my work? Have I ministered where I am—in the local church, and outside in other ministries and opportunities?

"In conclusion I am persuaded that the whole subject of missionary methods demands at this time [1899, but at any time] a fair, courteous and thorough discussion. Among the young especially there is a deep interest in the subject, and it is essential that sound and scriptural views should be adopted, applicable alike to the foreign field and to all forms of Christian work at home. While it is well that there should be such variety of organization and method as shall meet all views and utilize all resources, one thing seems certain: if the world is to be evangelized the burden of duty must rest upon all— upon those who go and those who stay. The support of the former must evolve upon the later, and it is the only way in which they can bear a substantial part. If the missionary's salary is a needless or questionable device, then the great majority of Christian people are exempt from any duty in the case, for it is impossible that all shall go, and the question, 'How shall they preach except they be sent?' is without meaning."[7]

Full-time Work Requires Full-time Support (Verses 4–6)

"Aren't we allowed to eat and drink? May we not travel with a Christian wife like the other messengers, like other Christian brothers, and like Cephas? Are Barnabas and I the only ones not allowed to leave their ordinary work to give time to the ministry?"

Do you sense the frustration Paul and Barnabas are feeling? The church at Corinth was supporting other apostles, but not him and Barnabas. They have come to the point where working and ministry are not compatible. He goes on:

Partnership Endorsed by Law (Verses 7–9)

"Just think for a moment. Does any soldier ever go to war at his own expense? Does any man plant a vineyard and have no share in its fruits? Does the shepherd who tends the flock never taste the milk? This is, I know, an argument from everyday life, but it is a principle endorsed by the Law. For is it not written in the Law of Moses: Thou shalt not muzzle the ox when he treadeth out the corn?"

Through this series of questions Paul uses army life, the farmer, the rancher, and even the ox to support the argument that Christian workers should receive support. These are, as he calls them, *"arguments from everyday life."*

Have you ever wondered if God really meant for Christian workers to have full support? The apostle states in these certain terms, an unequivocal, "Yes!" Even law (natural law and Old Testament law) supports the principle. The lesson for us is not to doubt God's intentions but to know his ways as revealed through His Word, particularly the portion we are reviewing right now.

So far Paul has built his case in three ways: from the genuineness of their lives and ministry to the Corinthians; from natural law (the soldier, farmer, and rancher); and from Old Testament law, the law of the ox. He is not finished.

The Right to Partnership (Verses 10–12)

Does God want missionaries to have full support?

"Now does this imply merely God's care for oxen, or does it include his care for us too? Surely we are included! You might even say that the words were written for us. For both the ploughman as he ploughs, and the thresher as he threshes should have some hope of an ultimate share in the harvest. If we have sown for you the seed of spiritual things need you be greatly perturbed because we reap some of your material things? And if there are others with the right to have these things from you, have not we an even greater right? Yet we have never exercised this right and have put up with all sorts of things, so that we might not hinder the spread of the gospel."

What assuring words these are to the Christian worker: *Surely we* [the "we" here is Paul and Barnabas, full-time Christian workers who were not sufficiently supported] *are included! You might even say that the words were written for us.* So, Christian worker, don't doubt God's purposes in this domain of your life. He does intend that you be supported—that you can leave your ordinary work and give full-time to the ministry.

The Law of the Temple (Verses 13–14)

"These words were written for us."

"Are you ignorant of the fact that those who minister sacred things take part of the sacred food of the Temple for their own use, and those who attend the altar have their share of what is placed on the altar? On the same principle the Lord has ordered that those who proclaim the gospel should receive their livelihood from those who accept the gospel."

Those to whom we minister here at home should be those who also are interested in sending us on to minister ["proclaim"] somewhere else. Again, the principle is grounded in Old Testament teaching—like the Law of the Ox. Numbers chapter eighteen is a good place to see the Old Testament teaching on this subject, embedded in the law of the Temple.[9]

The apostle has now stacked seven arguments:

1. Their genuine ministry to the Corinthians.
2. Full-time ministry requires full support.
3. Natural law: soldier, farmer, and rancher.
4. They were only claiming their rights.
5. Old Testament law: the rights of the ox.
6. Natural law: the rights of the sower.
7. Old Testament law: the temple

And Yet, A Higher Principle (Verses 16–18)[10]

"But I have never used any of these privileges, nor am I writing now to suggest that I should be given them. Indeed I would rather die than have anyone make this boast of mine an empty one! For I take no special pride in the fact that I preach the gospel. I feel compelled to do so; I should be utterly miserable if I failed to preach it. If I do this work because I choose to do so then I am entitled to a reward. But if it is no choice of mine, but a sacred responsibility put upon me, what can I expect in the way of reward? This, that when I preach the gospel, I can make it absolutely free of charge, and need not claim what is my rightful due as a preacher."

"But I have never used any of these privileges."

Even after all of these principles asserting the argument for support from the Corinthians, the apostle states a still higher principle: verses fifteen and nineteen.

Verse fifteen: *"But I have never used any of these privileges, nor am I writing now to suggest that I should be given them. Indeed I would rather die than have anyone make this boast of mine an empty one!"*

Verse nineteen: *"What can I expect in the way of reward? This, that when I preach the gospel, I can make it absolutely free of charge, and need not claim what is my rightful due as a preacher."*

His ministry was *free of charge.* He said, *I have never used any of these privileges....* What's the lesson—the application?

"Go to give and not to get."

Serve with no strings attached. Go to give and not to get. Never demand support. Your ministry and service must be just as free as was the apostles'. You must be free in spirit to minister with no expectations.

But why could Paul preach without charge? Only if he worked, or if God's people sent and supported him.

Never have to put a price on your service. This is the higher principle.

"Never put a price on your service."

God will see to it that the Christian worker who does his part receives his wage. For God has said: *"The laborer is worthy of his hire."* In a coming chapter, The Partnership Model, the Christian worker's part is explained.

I started out this chapter with the idea that belief systems determine attitudes, and that combination produces actions. The apostle Paul's actions, attitudes, and beliefs (teaching) are clear. The Holy Spirit put all of this in place for our learning, our encouragement and our action.

The apostle appealed to the Corinthians on the basis of his ministry to them. This was no sales pitch. He had a legitimate right to raise the issue of their support. Paul and Barnabas had served the Corinthian church. Paul's entire argument is based upon the demonstration of ministry—ministry to the Corinthians, themselves. The fruit of ministry among the Corinthians was the evidence justifying his request.

Ministry—service—in a local church and in the lives and ministries of others is the critical principle. How could missionaries expect God's people to send them to some other place to serve if they had not demonstrated their spiritual gifts and Christian virtues, and willingness to serve. In short, earning the right to be selected, supported, and sent. What mission agency would want someone who didn't come with this kind of spiritual track record?

"If you won't miss them we don't want them."

If you make the teachings of Scripture the key reference point, your internal guidance system will have the right information from which to produce and adjust your attitudes. Appropriate attitudes determine productive actions. You won't miss the target.

Hudson Taylor said, "God's work done in God's way never lacks God's supply."

What is God's way?

In the next chapter we will examine a model developed from the biblical principles given in this chapter.

It is not a model showing what God will do, or what God's people will or should do. It is a model that shows what a missionary should be and do.

END NOTES

[1] Frank F. Ellinwood, *"Questions and Phases of Modern Missions,"* Dodd, Mead and Company, 1899, p. 149.

[2] Polly C. Dye and Margaret Heppe, *"In His Glad Service: The Story of Royal and Eva Dye,"* Eugene, Oregon, Northwest Christian College, 1975, pp. 27–28.

[3] Using the word "formula" might imply to the reader that beliefs, attitudes, and actions work through a process that is mechanical in nature. Please note that the relationship of these human factors are diagramed as a chemical formula: implying the interrelated, and dynamic nature of the interrelationship among the factors. For in fact, human beings don't operate in mechanical ways—we are not robots. Beliefs, attitudes, and actions are so interrelated and interactive within us that it is difficult to always know where and when a particular factor begins and leaves off.

[4] Milton Rokeach, *Beliefs, Attitudes, and Values: A Theory of Organization and Change,* San Francisco: Jossey-Bass, 1969; and Milton Rokeach, *The Nature of Human Values,* New York: The Free Press, A division of Macmillan Publishing Company, Inc. 1973. Rokeach, in addition to publishing his own research, includes extensive bibliographies.

[5] Ellinwood, *Questions and Phases,*p. 146.

[6] Archibald Thomas Robertson, *"Word Pictures In The New Testament: The Gospel According To Luke,"* Grand Rapids, Baker Book House, 1930, Volume III, p. 296.

[7] Ellinwood, *Questions and Phases,* p. 152.

[8] Ellinwood, *Questions and Phases,* p. 148.

[9] When the apostle Paul refers to the economy of the Temple workers as a metaphor, Numbers eighteen (NIV) is one place where we can explore the basis of this metaphor. Note that remuneration was regular, and it was a wage returned to them for their work. Only some of the statements in Numbers eighteen are quoted.

I am giving you the service of the priesthood as a gift.

*All the holy offerings the Israelites give me I give to you and your sons as your portion and **regular** share.*

Everything in Israel that is devoted to the LORD is yours.

It is an everlasting covenant of salt before the LORD for both you and your offspring.

*I give to the Levites all the tithes in Israel as their inheritance **in return for the work** they do while serving at the Tent of Meeting.*

When you receive from the Israelites the tithe I give you as your inheritance, you must present a tenth of that tithe as the LORD's offering.

*You and your households may eat the rest of it anywhere, for **it is your wages for your work** at the Tent of Meeting.*

Ellinwood, *Questions and Phases,* p. 138, comments: *Now it so happened by way of divine example that God's own method of supporting the Levitical priesthood was thoroughly organized and systematic. It was proportionate, fixed, and compulsory. No more faith was required of the priest at the altar than of the shepherd among his flocks. Hardly any other man in the nation was quite so sure of a regular support as he.*

[10] When the devil tempted Jesus (Matthew chapter four) he *took him to the holy city and had him stand on the highest point of the temple. "If you are the Son of God,"* he said, *"throw yourself down. For it is written: He will command his angels concerning you, and they will lift you up in*

their hands, so that you will not strike your foot against a stone." Jesus answered him, "It is also written: Do not put the Lord your God to the test." This was a legitimate promise from the Psalms regarding the Lord's safety. Why did Jesus refuse to jump? What is the application? Because we are not (just as Jesus was not) to be presumptuous with God. Jesus brought a higher principle to bear on the situation which overrode the promise the devil quoted. That is what the apostle Paul is doing at this point in first Corinthians. May we be as wise.

11 Michael C. Griffiths, *Get Your Church Involved In Missions,* Belmont, The Vine, Sevenoaks, Kent TN13 3TZ, OMF Books, 1981, p. 33. I began from a different point than Michael Griffiths and from a different perspective, but found my thinking merging with his at several places. His two booklets, *Get Your Church Involved In Missions* and *Who Really Sends The Missionary,* Chicago, Moody Press, 1972 are excellent material: thought provoking and seminal. With Ellinwood, *Questions and Phases of Modern Missions,* 1899, who is quoted several times, Griffiths is the only other writer I've read who challenges the church and missions at the deepest level of thinking about selecting, supporting and sending missionaries.

CHAPTER FIVE

• • • • • • • • •

The Partnership Model
Partners as Investors

"The so-called 'faith' policy with its valued stress upon 'dependence on God alone' may, to some extent, have been responsible for a neglect of the proper intimacy between sending congregations and missions."[1]

The telephone call came from the wife of a couple whom I had tried to help with their support-raising activities. Unfortunately, I hadn't been able to be of much help. They had the same problem that I struggled with, a self-defeating belief system. They just couldn't break free of the live-by-faith-alone ideology. I understood, oh how I understood, but I couldn't seem to communicate some of my new thinking in a helpful way.

They called because they were getting ready to leave for a three-month trip visiting friends, family, and churches. They wanted some ideas on what to do. I had already told them everything I knew, none of which they were able to put into action, but I agreed to meet. We set a day and time.

When I hung up the telephone, I turned to God in prayer. This couple had been faith missionaries for thirty-five years. They had never had full support. They wanted to return to an overseas assignment, but their organization wouldn't let them go this time without full support.

I told God that I was at a loss and had no idea how to help them. Would He give me some way to communicate better? After praying, I began to doodle on a piece of paper. I wrote down a few words representing some fundamental principles I'd been thinking about and connected those ideas with some lines.

The Partnership Model you will read about in the next two chapters began to take shape on that piece of paper. In fact, the next day when my friends came for the appointment, I drew a diagram and began to share with them what I thought raising support was really all about.

I believe the Holy Spirit led me in my thinking and doodling. Right there in my office this couple began to change their whole perspective on raising support, after thirty-five years. It was a breakthrough. When they left my office that day they were like two new people. They stopped in the doorway, looked back and said, "For the first time we understand what raising support is all about. And we can do it!"

"For the first time we understand what raising support is all about. And we can do it!"

You remember what Jesus said, "You shall know the truth and the truth shall set you free." Well, I witnessed it that day. They came back three months later with full support.

I believe this was all of the Holy Spirit, too, because I didn't produce this model by my own brain power. It just seemed to come together. I also believe it was of the Lord because so many missionaries have been blessed by this Partnership Model.

Let's take a look.

Every missionary wants intimacy, not just money. According to Webster's, *"intimacy implies a close association between two parties resulting from careful study or investigation, which culminates in a formal or informal agreement"* [partnership].

If there has been neglect of intimacy (partnership) between those who send and those who go, and there has been neglect, what can the missionary do to help correct the situation?

Practically, partnership in ministry occurs because someone, a church, a friend, a family member, decides to invest some of their spiritual assets in a specific missionary ministry.

Why does anyone invest in anything? Answering this question is the key to understanding how developing partners in ministry is accomplished. The **partnership model** presented in this chapter is an answer to that question.

Why does anyone invest in anything?

Missionaries who follow this partnership model are assured intimacy with God's people. They are assured of the prayer and financial partnership needed to pursue a missionary ministry. Why partnership?

P A R T N E R S H I P is the term that best describes the relationship between the one who is sent and the sender. Partners share mutual responsibility for the task. They share in the rewards of accomplishment. There is intimacy.

Partner-partnership is a biblical concept. When the apostle Paul spoke of his relationship to the Philippian church, he called it a partnership: *"In all my prayers for all of you, I always pray with joy because of your partnership in the gospel from the first day until now"* (Philippians 1:4–5).

The foundational meaning of the Greek word used by Paul *(koinonia: that which is in common)* is **mutuality**.

Mutual Interest
Mutual Trust
Mutual Investment
Mutual Liability
Mutual Risk
Mutual Benefit
Mutual Commitment
Mutual Effort
Mutual Engagement
Mutual Reward

Mutuality is the bonding agent of the partnership between missionaries and their friends.

Partnership is a developmental task. The missionary has a role to play. God expects him to do his part. Partners are not discovered; partners are developed. It's not by faith/prayer alone. *"Faith by itself, if it is not accompanied by action, is dead"* (James 2:17).

Partners are investors. Partners invest in three, not necessarily mutually exclusive, ways. Partners invest through prayer. Partners invest money. Partners invest through numerous other encouraging acts. For example, taking care of the family pet while the missionaries are traveling, or while on an extended assignment overseas, is an investment through encouragement. Encouragement is an umbrella term that encompasses all the other helpful things God's people do for missionaries.

Christians have **spiritual assets** to invest: prayer, money, and encouraging acts. When Christians invest spiritual assets in a ministry, they are partners.

Why does anyone invest in someone else?

Why does anyone invest in someone else? One reason: we invest because we **trust**. As is shown later, the partner's trust is in both the missionary and the mission agency.

How does a Christian worker demonstrate trustworthiness: the precursor to trust? If you were to ask a group of veteran missionaries why they believe the persons and churches supporting them chose to do so, the majority would give this kind of an answer: *Because they know me.* Intimacy!

Personal relationship is a key ingredient in partnership development. As people and churches get to know the missionary, trust is built. People and churches invest in someone they trust. Partnership follows trust. Trust relationships are based primarily upon character: who the person is and the quality of spiritual life.

But trust alone is not sufficient. Partnership also follows

value. There must be, on the part of the missionary or prospective missionary, a demonstration of value. There must be evidence of spiritual value or who would invest? It was value that Paul so wonderfully and clearly demonstrated to the church at Corinth, as recorded in 1 Corinthians, chapter nine.

If trustworthiness is demonstrated primarily through personal relationships, how is value demonstrated?

Parenthetically, it needs to be said that in real life trust and value cannot be so neatly separated. These two dynamics of relationship and life are intertwined in ways that would make them hard to distinguish as separate influences in any given situation. They are distinguished in the Partnership Model for the purposes of understanding. Let's look at value.

Value is demonstrated through service and ministry. Service and ministry are almost synonymous terms in the New Testament. It could be said Christians minister through serving.

"As each of you has received a gift (a particular spiritual talent, a gracious divine endowment), employ it for one another as [befits] good trustees of God's many-sided grace—faithful stewards of the extremely diverse [powers and gifts granted to Christians by] unmerited favor" (1 Peter 4:10, Amplified NT).

"Likewise you that are younger and of lesser rank be subject to the elders—the ministers and spiritual guides of the church, giving them due respect and yielding to their counsel. Clothe (apron) yourselves, all of you, with humility in the garb of a servant, so that its covering cannot possibly be stripped from you..." (1 Peter 5:5, Amplified NT).

A missionary demonstrates value in two ways: through personal acts of service, and through the spiritual significance of the missionary task the missionary does, or will do.

Personal acts of service means the Christian worker is a servant. It can mean serving through preaching, teaching, etc., but not necessarily those two spiritual gifts. Service to others should

"Trust alone is not sufficient."

be a lifestyle, not limited in expression through spiritual gifts, alone.

One missionary discovered this broader meaning of service when he and his wife went on a ministry trip. They had been taught the Partnership Model with an emphasis on demonstrating value through service. On this particular trip, they decided not to seek speaking engagements; they would take them, when situations opened up, but their commitment and prayer was to seek opportunities to serve.

At their first stop on the trip they visited a family who were already supporting them. These partners were in the midst of painting their house. The missionary couple, following through on their commitment to serve, stayed long enough to help paint the house. Nothing about money was mentioned until the missionary couple was leaving. Then it was their friends following them to the car, who said, "We're going to increase the amount of support we are giving you."

Undoubtedly different conclusions could be drawn from this anecdote. But knowing the couple and the circumstances it was justifiable to conclude that relationships (trust) and service (value) were key ingredients in the response of these friends. Because these friends were already partners, it was a case of trust reinforced, and the continued demonstration of value, through an act of service.

Remember the apostle Paul's statements in 1 Corinthians chapter nine? *"But I have never used any of these privileges...and when I preach the gospel, I can make it absolutely free of charge, and need not claim what is my rightful due as a preacher."*

The service described in this model is service with no strings attached: no expectation of being paid back. The missionary couple who helped paint their friends' house was later asked, "Did you do that because you expected or hoped your friends would respond in a financial way?" "No!" they responded. "We committed ourselves to serve, and we asked God for opportunities to be servants."

You see, people who build relationships with others, and who serve others without strings, do not need to worry about money. Through relationship trust is established. Through service value is demonstrated. People and churches invest in someone they trust and value.

Of course, the word value refers specifically to spiritual value. Friends, family, and churches are investing in the spiritual value they see in missionaries: spiritual value demonstrated through good works, and the use of spiritual gifts. Friends, family, and churches would be remiss in their obligations if they selected and sent to missionary service people who had not demonstrated spiritual value here at home.

Demonstrating value has another dimension. Earlier, it was stated that the value of what the missionary is doing or will do on assignment must be of demonstrable value. It is relatively easy for the evangelist, Bible teacher, preacher, or Bible translator to talk about the value of their ministry. It is not so easy for the secretary, bookkeeper, computer programmer, or others in supporting roles.

The ability to not only be spiritually valuable at home, but to demonstrate the value of the ministry the missionary is going away to do, is a significant factor in the partnership process.

Why should anyone invest in a bookkeeper? Some might say they are not real missionaries. Anyone who is in a support role in missions has to be prepared to demonstrate the value of and perhaps defend their role as a missionary.

A missionary serving as a buyer and shipper in the U.S.A. (buying and shipping needed materials to overseas missionaries) understood the concept. In one of her newsletters, she had a photo of a missionary sitting at a table working alongside a national in a missionary task. They were both using number two pencils, which could clearly be seen in the photo. This home-assigned missionary had a caption like this, "I packed and shipped those number 2 pencils." She made the connection, for her partners, between her ministry and the results on the field.

One missionary couple who served one term as student residence parents wanted to return to the mission field. Two or three years had gone by since their first term; so, they were starting over in raising support. At about 50% they hit the wall. In a problem-solving discussion, they were asked, "What's your message? That is, when you have an opportunity to share your ministry with a church or with a small group, what are you saying?"

The answer was revealing. "Well, because we've already been on the mission field we have a slide presentation about our mission's ministry, and the results in people coming to Christ and churches being planted."

Sounds good, doesn't it? They were then asked, "When do you tell about being student residence parents? When and how do you explain your ministry?"

"Well, we don't say much about it because we think people want to know about those other kinds of results. That's the real mission."

When this couple changed their presentations to include more about their ministry—why student residence parents were important, the results in the lives of children to whom they ministered, the ministry to the missionary parents who had had to leave their children, and increased results in the parent's ministry—they began to see more people interested in a partnership with them.

People and churches want to know what the missionary's own ministry will be. Even though a supporting role, it is the missionary's specific ministry that people and churches will invest in.

Assessing Your value:
1. What do you do as a missionary, or will do?
2. Where will you be assigned?
3. In what specific way(s) is your assignment important to the overall ministry of the missionary organization?
4. Why you and not someone else? Why you and not your best friend, or someone else from your church?
5. What do you (will you) bring to this ministry that is unique, or valuable?
6. What would be the consequences to you personally if you don't get to go, stay or return?
7. What would be the consequences to the mission or ministry if you don't get to go, stay, or return?

Is a support worker really a missionary? This is and will probably remain, one of the most important questions a support worker has to face. If you have wondered about it, consider this analogy.

Every person who wears the uniform of a Marine, is a Marine. It doesn't matter if they are on the beaches with a rifle, behind the lines cooking food, preparing ammunition, keeping records, doing public relations, etc., they are a Marine.

Every role in the military is necessary. Some say it takes ten supporting soldiers to keep one man in the trenches. The ratio is far more striking and significant if the people back home are taken into account. In principle, that's the way it is in missions.

Support missionaries, though, must be convinced of the value of their roles, and be able to present—to demonstrate—the value of their roles.

"Is a support worker really a missionary?"

Anyone who is selected and sent to join the **Missionary Corps** is a missionary. If you have been selected to wear the missionary uniform, no matter your role, wear your uniform with honor and with authority.

It's the missionary, first and foremost, in whom the investment is made. It's their ministry that must be seen as having a value worth investing in. Fundamentally, it is the missionary who built the trust and who demonstrates the value (at home and on assignment).

I've asked numerous missionaries: "If you were to leave the organization that you serve with to join a different ministry, how many of your partners would go with you?" The universal answer is, "Almost all, if not all, of my partners would stay with me."

An organization once put this to the test. When a missionary left the mission for some reason, the organization wrote to all the missionary's partners and asked them to support another missionary in that organization.

Interestingly enough, when this was tried, the response was almost nil, but to some observers, not unexpected.

It simply shows that personal relationship is a foundational issue in the mind and heart of the investor. It shows personal relationship is more important than with whom the missionary serves.

By the way, it doesn't work even when a resigning missionary asks his long-term partners to transfer their giving to another missionary. The record shows there is very little response to this kind of effort. It might work better if the resigning missionary took the other missionary to meet those partners, to spend time with them, and to build a personal relationship.

"God's people like to invest in someone they know."

People and churches are going to primarily invest in the missionary, not in the organization with which they serve. It's the missionary who has the burden of demonstrating trustworthiness and of demonstrating value.

However, the organization, even though not primary, must also have a history of trustworthiness and value in the eyes of the Christian public. Every Christian knows the disastrous effect when ministries or leaders of ministries fail in a significant moral issue; that is, when trust is broken.

Organizations must be able to show results in ministry. Not instantaneous spiritual results, but a record of commitment to and pursuit of spiritual outcomes, and a record of results in harmony with the type of ministry and the political/cultural/spiritual context in which the ministry is carried out. Christians have a real and valid expectation that spiritual goals will be reached: people saved, churches planted, translations of the Bible completed, etc. But those expectations must be tempered by reality.

Missionaries are fortunate when they belong to an organization that has a faithful track record, a long history of obedience in the same direction. All of the faithful missionaries who have gone before them, who have laid that track, are passing on a wonderful and valuable legacy.

Every Christian worker who expects the support of God's people must be engaged in a local fellowship, or church. The word *engaged* means there is active participation in the life and ministry of the church, in the lives of the people of God. It means missionaries, when available, function within an environment where spiritual gifts are being exchanged—using their gifts to build up that local body of believers and also receiving the benefit of the spiritual gifts of others.

The missionary is engaged, not a spectator. Parenthetically, even though the word *engaged* is used to identify the special relationship a missionary has with at least one local church, the principle of engagement is also inherent in the concepts: Personal Relationships and Service/Ministry.

The local church is the central agent in sending missionaries.

The local church has fundamental responsibilities that cannot be delegated. When the Holy Spirit, in Acts thirteen, said to the prophets and teachers at Antioch, *"Set apart for me Barnabas and Saul for the work to which I have called them,"* He, the Holy Spirit, was modeling a procedure—a process— for the church to follow in its role as primary selector and sender.

"The local church has fundamental responsibilities that cannot be delegated."

The prophets/teachers responded to the Holy Spirit's selection of Barnabas and Paul. They laid their hands on them, submitting to the Holy Spirit's choice. This incident in Acts thirteen is never repeated exactly like this again. But in the book of Acts particularly, the process of selection and sending by the local church is repeated. In fact, this process was in place before the Acts thirteen event, which will be shown later.

It seems highly significant that it was the apostle Paul who was being processed by the local church at the Holy Spirit's instigation. The apostle Paul had the most dramatic calling of any New Testament believer. His calling came from, accompanied by dramatic circumstances, the mouth of the Lord Jesus Christ, Himself.

If there ever was a person who could have been considered a special case—didn't need the local church to select, or to send him—it was this apostle. Yet we see the Holy Spirit instituting local church authentication.

This same process, long before the Antioch event, can be seen in the choosing of the seven men who were to distribute relief supplies. *"Brothers, choose seven men from among you...known to be full of the Spirit and wisdom."* The ensuing process *"pleased the whole group" (Acts 6:3–5)*. Note here how the leaders delegated to the congregation who should be chosen. *"They* (the congregation) *chose Stephen, a man full of faith and of the Holy Spirit; also Philip,"* etc. *"They* (the congregation) *presented these men to the apostles, who prayed and laid their hands on them."*

The process reappears in Acts 15:22, "Then the apostles and elders, with the whole church, decided to choose some of their own men and send them to Antioch with Paul and Barnabas." Note how the *"whole church"* was involved here, and the *"whole group"* as in Acts six.

The Holy Spirit is, again, as in Acts thirteen, a definite part of this process, *"It seemed good to the Holy Spirit and to us...."* (Acts 15:28). *"The men* [then] *were sent off...."* (Acts 15:30).

It is significant and instructive that in all the sendings in Acts, the emphasis made in Scripture is never upon an individual volunteering or upon his own subjective sense of call, but always at the initiative of others.

No one selected themselves.

Yes, it is legitimate and necessary for a missionary to have a strong sense of personal leading from the Lord, and it is often necessary for a mission agency to qualify the missionary candidate for a specific role in that agency, but these two elements are not sufficient. This third element, selection, at the local church level, with the Holy Spirit superintending all along the way, is the only sure way to know God's leading.

The process described above, the involvement of a local church, is normative: the general case. There could be unusual situations: the special case that does not follow the pattern presented in these passages. However, in working with hundreds of missionaries over a twenty-year period of time, I have yet to find a person who is successful (has and maintains adequate financial support) who has not had strong roots in at least one local church. The pattern is consistent. Actually, most well-supported missionaries have roots in more than one church.

Missionaries must act rightly toward the local church. "*Likewise you that are younger and of lesser rank be subject to the elders— the ministers and spiritual guides of the church, giving them due respect and yielding to their counsel...*" (1 Peter 5:5, Amplified).

There are veteran missionaries (home assigned, or on furlough) who do not have adequate financial support. In many cases, when working with them on the problem, what has been observed is they are not engaged in a local church. They go to a local church, but they are not engaged there. They have no ministry or point of service in the church. This has also been observed with many young people who are considering missions.

Anyone who is seeking to serve God in missions, but who doesn't have a solid relationship with at least one local church, should be told:

Stop! Go home! Don't go another step further until you have the blessing of a local body of believers who know you and through whom the Holy Spirit has placed His hand of blessing on this decision.

The local church should have at least these domains of interest and involvement:

1. Take initiative in and confirm the selection and training of their missionaries.

2. Provide prayer, financial, and encouraging partnership.

3. Assist in building a broader-based constituency, if this church cannot provide all of the resources.

4. Continue encouragement through letters and visits, and by other acts of involvement: telephone calls, e-mails, faxes, and Christmas presents, etc.

5. Hold the missionary accountable for results based upon understood and agreed-upon standards relevant to this particular missionary ministry.

6. Establish a missionary care team that is responsible for carrying out the churches' responsibilities while the missionary is on assignment, and while the missionary is on furlough.

7. When a missions agency is involved, work with appropriate agency leadership in major decisions, and accountability.

Whether veteran missionary or only at the interest level, being engaged in service in a local church/fellowship/assembly is fundamental. The missions agency must allow for, literally insist upon, this process being established and maintained by the church.

"The mission agency must insist on the process."

Missionaries and missions agencies defeat their own purposes if this process is allowed to short circuit.

One veteran missionary, while home on furlough, made the decision to give the majority of his free time to service in his home church. He told the pastor he would be available for three days each week for several months.

The missionary's thought was that the pastor would want him to serve on the missions committee, teach a Sunday school class on missions, and maybe even preach a sermon or two on missions.

The pastor was delighted to have him, but not for the reasons the missionary anticipated. Not once was he asked to speak about missions, or even be on the missions committee. He painted a Sunday school room, ran errands, worked in the church office, etc. The missionary became the pastor's gopher.

At the end of furlough, the pastor told the missionary the church wanted to have a Sunday evening that was just for him and his family. It so happens the missionary family still didn't have all of the support needed to return to their assignment. The pastor knew about it. The evening service was planned and the pastor presented the missionary's financial needs to the congregation.

The response overwhelmed this missionary family. All of their financial needs were met that night. Later that evening, the missionary exclaimed to the pastor, "I just don't understand how this happened. We are overwhelmed with the response. Why? Why did the congregation respond like this?"

The pastor replied, "Don't you know why? What have you been doing for these last few months? I'll tell you. You've been actively serving the people of this church while you've been serving me. Do you realize how many in this congregation have gotten to know you over the last few months?"

A furloughing missionary might be reading this and wondering how he, with so many other items on his agenda, could possibly give any extended time in ministry to supporting churches. This is a real problem. The only solution is that missionaries and missions agencies are going to have to allow churches to have some part in furlough planning.

Churches, when presented with the facts, will work with missionaries and agencies in developing realistic and acceptable plans. But to leave churches out of furlough planning is shortsighted. Some will want to be intimately involved and some will not, but it is important to allow for involvement.

Local churches have the responsibility to select and to send. Wise missionaries involve their churches in major decision making at the beginning and throughout their careers. Wise missionaries maintain accountable relationships. Wise missionaries enjoy the prayer partnership of their supporting churches.

What should missionaries be most concerned about in the process of partnership? These three things: relationships, service and selection. If missionaries focus on these three ideas—build relationships, serve with no strings attached and submit to selection—they will build trust and value. Individuals, families, and churches will want to invest in these kinds of people.

These aspects of partnership are the missionary's job; they don't represent what God will do. This is the missionary's part. Yes, the missionary needs to ask God's help to carry out that part, but it is the missionary's to carry out.

"Think principle." The selection step will not occur exactly like it did for anyone in the book of Acts. But think principle here. If you are a missionary or considering missions, be the kind of person (trust) doing the kinds of things (value) that will cause God's people—whether church or individual—to say, "You've got the right stuff. We think you should be involved in Christian work."

Now, they may never voice this to you, and it may be your initiative that causes them to entertain these thoughts, but it's their observation, involvement and their conclusion that's important.

It's OK for a person to take the initiative and to say to church leadership, "I believe the Lord is leading me into missions, and I am interested in joining X, Y, Z mission organization." But, that needs to be followed up with this question, "What do you think?"

Every missionary should be allowing the principle of selection to be at work in his support-raising activities. Allow for time in relationships and time for opportunities to serve/minister for the principle of selection to be working. Even if churches and people never voice to the missionary, *"We select you"* the missionary needs to be available, and give time for this aspect of the support-raising process to occur, even if it is subjective.

The selected missionary will be the sent missionary.

The selected missionary will be the one with whom people will covenant to be prayer partners. The selected missionary will be the one who experiences churches and people joining the team as financial partners. The selected missionary will experience lots of encouragement.

Selected missionaries have obligations too. They have the obligation to consult their partners on all major decisions. They are obligated to some form of accountability, even if just regular newsletters in which reports of the work are included.

The selected missionary will be sent with sufficient partnership, and will be honoring that partnership with reciprocal input and feedback to those partners.

This is a partnership based upon spiritual authority, and spiritual integrity. It is a partnership that produces spiritual strength. The selected missionary is sent in spiritual strength, not weakness. Adequate finances are a legitimate aspect of spiritual strength. However, finances are only one of the expected outcomes.

If missionaries think their job is to raise money, they don't understand the job requirements of building a partnership team. If they think it's to have a super-abundant, powerful faith, they don't understand. After all, how many Christians have that kind of faith? Faith like that is a gift. We are told clearly in Scripture that the gifts are distributed as the Holy Spirit wills: *"All these are the work of one and the same Spirit, and he gives them to each one, just as he determines"* (1 Corinthians 13:11). *"Are all apostles?*

"The selected missionary will be the sent missionary."

It is a partnership of strength.

• **89** • • • • • • • •

Are all prophets? Are all teachers? Do all work miracles? Do all have gifts of healing? Do all speak in tongues? Do all interpret?" (1 Corinthians 13:29–30).

Do all have wonder-working faith?

If the gift of faith was a necessary requirement for being a missionary, there wouldn't be many missionaries. The idea goes against the principle of the body of Christ being made up of people with many gifts. The gift of faith isn't a requirement for having adequate financial resources, any more than a requirement for membership in the body of Christ.

The Partnership Model is a strong model. It is strong for these reasons:

1. The wide application of its concepts: application in other domains of human activity, not just in partnership development. The effectiveness of a ministry of witnessing is dependent upon demonstrating trust and value. The witness must establish a relationship, must be engaged in the life of the person with whom Christ is to be shared, and must be a servant to that person. A person will want to believe in the Christ who is presented this way. These concepts are widely applicable in the secular world as well. For example, people invest in companies or enterprises where there is a sense of trust and the expectation of value. It is axiomatic.

2. All the significant variables are encompassed in the model. When stage one, presented in this chapter, is coupled with stage two (the chapter *The Partner As Owner*), most, if not all of the variables are accounted for. Some variables are inherent in major points of the model and are not necessarily identified in the diagrams.

3. No particular spiritual gift is required. Anyone can build relationships. Anyone can serve others. Anyone can be engaged in a church. You don't have to be able to sing, preach, teach, or have the gift of faith. You don't have to be an effective salesper-

"The GIFT of faith isn't a requirement for having adequate financial resources, any more than a requirement for membership in the body of Christ."

son. Your spiritual gifts are valid in any fellowship or relationship. Your acts of service will demonstrate value. In short, anyone can build trust and anyone can demonstrate value.

4. A support worker (bookkeeper, secretary, builder, etc.) can do partnership development following the Partnership Model. You don't have to be an evangelist, preacher, pilot, teacher, or translator. Support workers can build relationships, be engaged, and maintain a lifestyle of service. This model shows the way for anyone.

5. Place of assignment—overseas or home assigned—doesn't matter. If you are a servant, doing the kinds of things presented in this model, where you are going to serve God will not be a major issue. If it is an issue, it will be because of factors that are outside the domain of the model. For example, a church may have a policy that it supports only those who do church planting, or it supports only those who serve overseas.

A dose of reality is needed at this point. Let's go back to the formula:

Beliefs →Attitudes → Actions. Another factor needs to be added to make the formula complete: Beliefs →Attitudes → Actions → Context.

Context is the crucible in which one's beliefs, attitudes, and actions are played out in real life. Every missionary candidate or veteran operates within a distinct context. Some have deep roots in a denominational background. Some have a long history of family involvement in Christianity: maybe there's an uncle who is a pastor; a sister who is on the missions committee of another church; or Mom and Dad are charter members of a large missions-minded church.

To contrast, some missionary candidates have no deep spiritual roots anywhere. They haven't even been Christians very long. People who fit this profile should make it their priority to establish themselves in a church. God's people should have the opportunity to exercise their responsibility to select, and to have a part in sending and sustaining all missionaries. Missionaries need to earn the right to be selected, and earn the right to be sent.

One couple decided to follow this advice. They did have a home church. The leadership of the church was asked by the missionary couple, "What would you like us to do in order to have this church be our sending church?" The leadership said, "Because of your lack of experience in ministry that we have observed, we would like you to give three years in ministry here at the church. Then, we will decide what the church will do."

The husband said three years later, just before leaving for an overseas assignment, "Those three years were the best thing we could have done. We are leaving with full support, three years of ministry experience, a sense of being ready, and a church that is completely behind us. We wouldn't have had it any other way! We really weren't ready and our church leadership knew it."

Even though not said, the mission agency that this couple serve with could not help but be happy that this missionary team arrived with experience in ministry, more mature, and fully supported.

There are some denominational churches that do not support independent, faith missions. What does the candidate do who comes from a church with this tradition?

Some churches just aren't missions-minded. Some churches give only to missionaries and missions that do certain kinds of ministry: evangelism and church planting, for example. Some churches send out their own missionary teams, and support no one else. What do candidates do with contexts like these?

Anyone considering missions must take a hard look at context. Realism must be exercised. If you attend a church that is denominationally oriented in its missions program, you may have to make some adjustments in your plans for partnership development.

Do not turn your back on this church. They can still be part of your prayer team. They can still have a ministry of encouragement. Some churches with a denominational tradition allow missionaries to develop partners within the congregation on an individual basis. It may mean you will have to seek out another place of fellowship. Be open to talk these things over with the pastoral staff and your friends.

The important thing is to know your personal history and context and to take it into consideration.

Context is a fundamental determiner of how long it takes to build a complete partnership team. For example, the candidate who comes from a long line of Christians; who grew up in a missions-minded church; who has numerous friends from Bible college days; who has a history of ministry in more than one church, will most often take far less time to raise support than the person whose background doesn't match this profile.

"How long does it take to raise support?"

There is a particular danger for the missionary who sees others getting their support quickly, as if with no effort, and comparing their personal experience with what he sees in others.

We are taught in the Scriptures "*But they, measuring themselves by themselves, and comparing themselves among themselves, are not wise*" (2 Corinthians 10:12b, KJV). Your context may mean you will have to spend more time than someone else doing the kinds of things explained in this book. Watch out for comparison; it's not wise.

Whether it's before you go, or after you've become a missionary, understand the task of partnership development: get engaged in a local church, share your spiritual gifts, serve people as a lifestyle (inside the church and outside), and build personal relationships.

Build trust; demonstrate value.

*"Don't try to send
yourself to the
mission field."*

People and churches invest in someone they trust and in someone they value. Don't try to send yourself to the mission field. Instead, submit to the selection/sending process established by the Holy Spirit. How else will God's people know if a particular missionary candidate has the qualities, gifts, skills, and experience needed on the mission field? How will the mission agency know? How will the prospect know?

End Notes

1   Michael C. Griffiths, *Get Your Church Involved In Missions*, 1981, OMF Books, p. 11.

2   *The Zondervan Pictorial Bible Dictionary*, Merrill C. Tenney, General Editor, 1967, Zondervan Publishing House, Grand Rapids, Michigan, under the topic fellowship, p. 282.

3   Even though unjustified, we find in 2 Corinthians, chapters eleven and twelve, that there were unresolved issues between Paul and the Corinthians. One of those issues was money and the Corinthians' trust in Paul and Titus was the concern. Paul says (facetiously) to the Corinthians, *"How were you inferior to the other churches, except that I was never a burden to you? Forgive me this wrong! Now I am ready to visit you for the third time, and I will not be a burden to you, because what I want is not your possessions but you.... Yet, crafty fellow that I am, I caught you by trickery! Did I exploit you through any of the men I sent you? I urged Titus to go to you and I sent our brother with him. Titus did not exploit you, did he? Did we not act in the same spirit and follow the same course?"* We see in this situation how lack of trust, although unjustified, was a key ingredient in lack of partnership between the church at Corinth and Paul.

4   The International Standard Bible Encyclopedia, General Editor, Geoffrey W. Bromiley, Grand Rapids, Michigan, William B. Eerdmans Publishing Company, 1990, Volume III (K–P, under the topic ministry), p. 365.

⁵ Michael C. Griffiths, *Who Really Sends The Missionary,* Chicago, Moody Press, 1974. An excellent booklet in which the role of the church in selecting and sending is justified, mainly from a Scriptural background, but also from a practical point of view. Particularly interesting and insightful are Griffith's comments on the inadequacies of the "volunteer system," p. 132. By volunteer system, Griffiths means the historical track record of individual and missions agency taking initiative in the selection/sending process based upon an individual's sense of "call," [volunteering] and the mission's need for workers. This booklet was originally published in England in 1972 by OMF books under the title "Get Involved in Missions!"

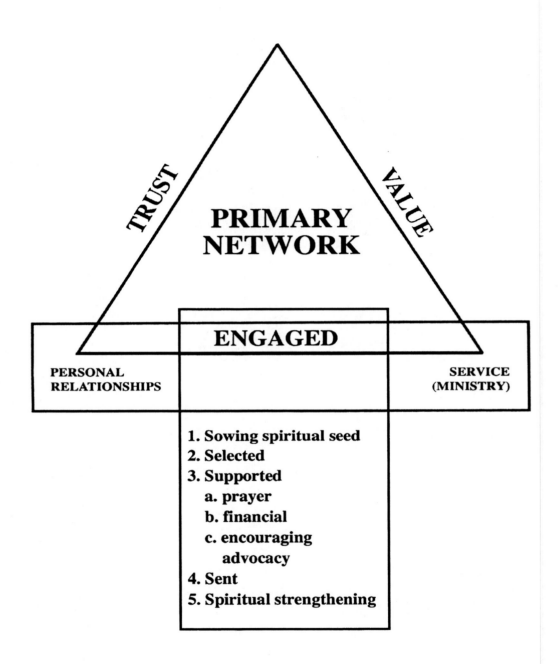

CHAPTER SIX
· · · · · · · ·

The Partnership Model
Partners As Owners

*"You know, this thing of raising support overwhelms me.
It seems impossible!"*

Those are the sentiments of many people who are faced with, for the first time in their lives, developing partners in ministry. Some veteran missionaries feel the same way.

Statements like the above are usually generated from a false expectation: *I'm the one with the burden of raising all this money. It's just God and me.*

Granted, anyone plus God is a mighty powerful combination. But it seems clear from Scripture that God intends it to be the missionary *and* the body of Christ. It can't be done alone, and God never intended that it be done alone. Missionaries need not feel alone in the partnership process.

"God never intended that building a partnership team be done alone."

Expectations like the ones expressed above are the reasons many missionaries make the mistake of thinking partnership development is a task for the strong and independent personality, or the person with great faith, or with great sales ability. The Lord makes it clear in the Scriptures that, *"From him the whole body, joined and held together by every supporting ligament, grows*

"Is raising support intended only for strong, daring personalities?"

and builds itself up in love, as each part does its work" (Ephesians 4:16).

"Partnership development is a team effort."

Partnership development is a team effort. Every missionary needs the help of God's people. Clearly, the Lord set up the parts of his body to function together in every part of its work, including missions.

In the last chapter, the **partnership model** was developed around the concept of partners as **investors**. In this chapter the model will be extended to include the concept of **ownership:** partners as owners.

Ownership is the second level of partnership.

In partnership development, it is necessary for the missionary to have some—not necessarily all—partners to be both investors and owners.

Ownership means that some partners will have a mindset expressed something like this: "The Browns' ministry is my ministry. When they leave for their assignment, I'm going with them. No, not in person, but through my prayers, my financial support, and encouragement. I have a stake in the Browns' ministry. Their success is my success. Their blessings, trials, challenges, and rewards are mine too. Jim and Debbie can't do it without me."

The prevailing characteristic of the **partner/owner** is a willingness to be involved—to own the missionary's challenges. We will focus mainly on the challenge of generating a complete partnership team.

This chapter is intended to be very practical. It is meant for missionaries, or prospective missionaries. If you fit one of these categories, you need to know there is work ahead.

You will be asked to do some deep and honest evaluation of yourself and your relationship to others. The information and insight you will gain about yourself and your existing network of relationships and partnerships will bring you closer to an understanding of your potential to develop a complete partnership team.

Let's start with a general question. Who is it among your close friends and family that would most likely **own** your missionary ministry?

That question can be answered in three ways: two are conceptual, and one quite specific. But first it will be helpful to have an identifying term for the people who are most likely to own one's ministry. Note that in the illustration the words **primary network** are added to the model.

A missionary's **primary network** is the people with whom the missionary already has a **high level** of **trust** and **value**. That is one conceptual way to identify who the owners might be.

A metaphor that might help is imagining a baseball player coming to the plate to bat. He is the last regular batter of the last inning of the game. If he gets a hit, his teammate on third base will score the winning run. As the batter takes his stance at the plate, he hears cheers from the stands: "Come on Charlie, you can do it! Just get a hit!" There is yelling and clapping accompanying the encouraging words to Charlie.

These **fans in the stands** are, by analogy, Charlie's primary network. They are the people who believe in him—who think he can do it. They are doing all they can within the context of a baseball game to help him succeed. Charlie has trust and value with them. A missionary's primary network is the fans in the stands. Even if not overtly understood, or expressed, primary network people have selected Charlie.

"Primary networks are fans in the stands."

The most practical way to identify your primary network is to write down the names of the people you believe are in your primary network. You are doing some educated guessing here.

Write down the names of ten people you believe are in your primary network, lots of trust and value in the bank, fans in the stands. Now consider this more practical way to identify your primary network using these criteria: they already give to your ministry; they pray regularly for your ministry; they have been strong encouragers.

By definition, primary network people are those who have already invested some of their spiritual assets in you.

If you don't have financial and prayer partners yet, then focus on the fans in the stands concept. Who are ten people that love you, have encouraged you to serve the Lord; who if they knew you wanted to be a missionary would say something like, "Yes, that's right; that's what you should do!" These people do not have to be geographically close to you or to one another.

Don't forget your pastor or missions committee. Are they fans in the stands?

If your pastor or missions committee are not behind you for any reason other than church mission policies (for example, they don't support the type of mission you are going to serve with) *Stop!* You are about to make a major spiritual mistake. Go back and read the previous chapter of this book before proceeding any farther.

Go on, if you fit the profile explained earlier.

Now that you have ten names of people you believe are members of your primary network, do the recommended evaluations. Let's start with the first person listed. Think back—when was the last time you saw or spoke with that person?

Why should you do this? It will help you answer three important questions:

1. What is my actual personal relationship with this person?
2. Do I need to renew, restore, or strengthen this relationship?
3. Should I put this person on my priority list of people to visit?

Why ask these questions? It brings us back to the partnership model, to the foundational issues of relationship and trust. You are evaluating your relationship with this one particular person, whether trust exists, and the level of that trust.

If you haven't seen this person for say, five years, and have not been in regular communication, you should not assume too much.

Veteran missionaries, who have maintained a strong linkage with their constituencies through written communication, can assume trust and value, but personal contact should be renewed at every opportunity.

In general, if you see this person regularly and he/she is part of your circle of friends, you can assume trust does exist. It doesn't mean they will be your partner—that is an assumption you can't make, nor should make.

It is probably a good time to point out you are not evaluating, at this point, a friend's potential for being a partner. You are evaluating the level of trust with this particular person. **This is a significant distinction.** It is really important to understand and agree with this distinction.

This is subjective, but answer this question, Has God used me in this person's life? What are you really analyzing here? Yes, it is value. Is this friend a witness to your spiritual value? Has he/she/they seen you in action? Would they agree that you have a legitimate portfolio of service and ministry?

Do you see how this exercise is really an evaluation of you?

If you are identifying a church as a member of your primary network, think of a significant person—pastor, missions committee member, good friend, etc. at that church and write that person's name on the line. You can write the church name in parenthesis.

You wrote the names of ten people. Maybe you have 50 or 100 in your primary network. Make a list of *all* their names. Now think about each one of them in terms of the quality of your relationship—when you last saw them, talked with them or wrote to them. And ask yourself, "Have I in any way served them?"

"You are living proof of God's call to me."
(1 Corinthians 9:3)

To the praise of the
Jesus Christ, not to get
money.

"Each one should use whatever gift he has received to serve others, faithfully administering God's grace in its various forms. If anyone speaks, he should do it as one speaking the very words of God. If anyone serves, he should do it with the strength God provides, so that in all things God may be praised through Jesus Christ..." (1 Peter 4:10–11).

In what ways can you serve? Yes, using the gift(s) you have received to serve others. But serving others can go outside of one's spiritual gift(s).

Administering God's grace in its various forms implies that grace comes in an abundance of forms, and should be administered in an abundance of ways. For example, babysitting the pastor's children so that he and his wife can enjoy an evening out. Washing windows, repairing things, doing dishes after the church social, helping paint someone's house, etc., are examples of ways to serve.

Peter also said, *"Indeed all of you should defer to one another and wear the [overall] of humility in serving each other"* (1 Peter 5:5, Phillips).

"Likewise you that are younger and of lesser rank be subject to the elders—the ministers and spiritual guides of the church, giving them due respect and yielding to their counsel. Clothe (apron) yourselves, all of you, with humility—as the garb of a servant, so that its covering cannot possibly be stripped from you..." (1 Peter 5:5, Amplified New Testament).

What does Peter (Phillip's paraphrase) mean by the *overall of humility?* It means, as is brought out in the Amplified, that humility dresses in work clothes; symbolically and figuratively, work clothes are the uniform of a servant.

That specific people will become partners cannot be guaranteed. Trust and value can be guaranteed, if you follow these principles. People invest in those they trust and in whom they have seen spiritual value; so don't worry about partners. If you are faithful to do your part, God will provide the partners.

One other thing can be guaranteed, the person who **does not** build relationships and who does not serve others, will not be building trust and value, and will never have adequate partnership.

You may find that you are in good shape as you evaluate yourself. **You have trust and value in the bank,** so to speak, with a lot of people. Great! But don't stop building trust and demonstrating value. Partnership development is a lifetime venture for the career missionary. Oh, and by the way, make sure to notice that it isn't money in the bank but trust and value, which are far more important than money.

Money comes through partners; partners come because they trust and because they value. As the old saying goes "Don't put the cart before the horse."

There are veteran missionaries who have been low on support who actually had a lot of trust and value in the bank with a number of people and churches, but who never drew on that trust and value. They never asked their friends for help when the going got financially tough.

Why don't some missionaries ask for help? Sometimes it is because of their belief system. They can't ask because their belief system says "It's by faith alone," and that means "Tell God only." Perhaps it is just plain old pride, or maybe stubbornness.

Why don't missionaries ask for help?

Ownership is the key idea in this chapter. You are engaged in the process of identifying the people (your primary network) who are most likely to express a sense of ownership of your ministry, move from investor to owner. By the evaluation you are doing so far, you have been evaluating yourself in relationship to your primary network.

One of the things missionaries have to do is provide oppor-

• **103** • • • • • • • •

tunities for ownership: encourage ownership. Two ideas that you might use to open the door of ownership are: Advocacy and Prayer/Advisory Council (PAC).

Advocacy is a global concept; that is, everyone listed as a member of your primary network is a potential advocate. The PAC is more limited. Only a few of your primary network will be able to participate as owners through a PAC.

Advocates are people who own your cause. Let's see how it might work.

You've already written down at least ten names of people whom you have reasons to believe are in your primary network.

Take a good look at the total illustration and the sample scenario.

Bob and Betty Bing are the names used in the example. Parenthetically, if you use the chart provided, it will be names of people from your own list that appear in the names column.

Continuing with the illustration, the Bings just received a letter from one of their missionary friends. It was a letter something like this (an advocacy letter):

Dear Bob and Betty,

You know how the Lord has been leading us to consider missionary service. We haven't forgotten your words of encouragement at the restaurant that night after church. And that financial gift you sent last month really helped.

As we've moved forward in this venture of faith, it has become more real to us that we need the help of God's people in a variety of ways. As you know, raising support is a big challenge. We are finding out we need a number of individuals, families, and churches to join as regular financial partners. It's estimated we will need about forty individuals and families, and as many as five churches to make up our complete partnership team.

The mission won't let us go to our assignment without a

complete team; so, this is a big item in our prayers, and it is an area with which we are going to need some help.

One of our family members, my brother Jim, spoke to his pastor about us. As a result, we have the opportunity to share our ministry and make some new friends at his church. We don't know if this will lead to a new church partner, but it is the kind of opportunity we need. We have to leave the results in God's hands.

We are wondering if you would pray about acting as an advocate for us (like Jim did) in one of your spheres of influence. There are ways to help other than what my brother did. We could speak in a Sunday school class, meet some of your friends at your house, share at a Bible study, etc. We have some other ideas of what we can do. We can discuss those with you at another time.

What we need are opportunities to meet new people and to share our ministry. People and churches need to get to know us first. Maybe partnership will follow should the Lord lead in that way.

One of us will call in a few days. We wanted you to have time to pray and to think about it. It is one way you might help, but if it is not comfortable to you, that's ok.

Our love,

Nathan and Nancy

This sample letter is an advocacy letter. It is the kind of letter that will open the door of ownership. Some people, like Jim, are spontaneous advocates; you don't have to ask. But many people, even though keenly interested in their missionary friend, will not think of being an advocate. But if asked, may very well respond positively.

Get accustomed to asking for help. You won't get to the mission field without it. Well, you might get there, but you probably won't stay.

Get accustomed to asking for help.

Don't attempt to engage anyone in an advocate role by writing them a letter unless you plan to make the follow-up telephone call. Maybe you have never taken this kind of action before and it scares you a little.

Consider this: *"After all, who in the ordinary way is likely to injure you for being enthusiastic for good? And if it should happen that you suffer [for righteousness sake], that is a privilege...simply concentrate on being completely devoted to Christ in your hearts"* (1 Peter 3:13–14, Phillips).

At the time of the call, Bob and Betty said, "Yes." They would pray about helping these missionary friends share their ministry in one of their (the Bings') spheres of influence.

Bob and Betty attend a Friday night Bible study. They felt free to tell this group about their missionary friends and to ask if the missionaries could have the opportunity to share on a Friday night. The group agreed.

Advocates are giving a very precious commodity to the missionary, their trust and value. Trust and value that they, the advocates, have built in their spheres of influence. The advocate is being vulnerable—taking a chance—investing a valuable asset in the missionary—their reputation.

Trust and Value are pervasive concepts. In fact, developing trust and value should be the major goal of an opportunity like speaking to a Friday night Bible study, Sunday school class, Sunday evening service, etc.

Do you know what the major goal would be of a lot of missionaries at this Friday night Bible study?

Their goal would be to make a crackerjack presentation, give a good talk, show a great video, or tell all about the wonderful ministry they are involved in. The missionary would be thinking that the group is going to be so blessed and inspired by my presentation that they (the group) will want to sign up and get involved.

This is a false expectation.

This kind of expectation on the part of missionaries is what causes many to say things like (after putting thousands of miles on their cars, speaking in several churches, and meeting with other groups and individuals), "**why** don't people respond? Those people (or churches) just don't care about missions anymore."

An opportunity to make a presentation, while good in and of itself, does not, in most cases, build trust and value. It will be a starter, and contribute mostly to demonstrating value, but it will not provide the elements for completing the whole process.

What is needed is to build a personal relationship(s) with a member(s) of the group, and to seek to be a servant (with no strings attached) to these individuals. Trust is built through relationships; value is demonstrated through service. People (churches) invest in someone they trust and value.

Going back to the Friday night Bible study, imagine the missionary with the major goal of starting a new relationship. Circulating during the social time, a conversation develops with a member of the group. A common interest is discovered. Bonding begins to take place. The missionary says, "You know one of the best things that's happened tonight is getting to meet you." The interest seems to be mutual. The missionary takes some initiative.

"I'm going to be here for two more days. Any chance we could get together again? How about tomorrow evening? If you put on the tea, I'll bring a dessert. "

What will happen when they get together? Will the missionary bring the dessert and his intention to sign them up as financial partners? No! This is a relationship beginning to form. Beware of presumption in building relationships.

What the missionary wants to bring besides the dessert is the intention to build a genuine relationship. If the relationship develops, there will also be opportunities to serve this person. In fact, the missionary should be asking God to grant him the privilege of serving these people in some personal way, with no strings attached: *"This is your spiritual [reasonable] act of service"* (Romans 12:1).

There will probably be an opportunity to add this person to your mailing list and to begin corresponding on a personal basis. If the relationship seems to be growing as you get together that first time, go ahead and say something like this: "We would really like to have you on our mailing list. It would help us to keep in touch with you, which we would really like to do. Would you like to receive our newsletter?"

People do not want a relationship with a ministry (impossible) they want a relationship with the missionary.

Too many missionaries are like a stone skipping across the pond—not penetrating the surface of people's lives—bouncing along to another meeting, and another.

Remember the Bings, the advocates who arranged the opportunity to speak to the Friday night Bible study? They could have been invited to be part of the tea and dessert get together. That would have been a natural arrangement. But if it didn't happen that way, be sure to tell the Bings about your new relationship with one of their friends.

Bob and Betty have been praying about this. They made the commitment to be your advocate. They are deeply interested in how the Lord worked. So, ask the Bings to invite your new friends over some evening. The Bings and your new friends have something new in common, friendship with you, and interest in your ministry. Your advocates have a vested interest in the long-term outcome of this relationship. They will help nurture it.

Go back to where you have ten names written down. Answer the question: Would this member of my primary network be open to receiving an advocacy letter from me? Realistically, you should be able to say "Yes" for almost every member of your

> *"People do not want a relationship with a ministry…they want a relationship with the missionary."*

> *Situations like these are fabrications for illustrative purposes. Relationship building, demonstration of value and selection cannot be scripted.*

primary network. These are people with whom you have a high level of trust and value, your fans in the stands. "No" is possible because exceptions exist.

Advocacy can take many forms. One missionary had a friend who lived on the back-bay in a wealthy area. Everyone who lived in this part of town had a yacht docked in their back yard. The friend put on a Saturday night party for the missionary and invited all of his friends. The flyer was an invitation to a barbecue, and told about the missionary and his needs for financial support and one-time expenses. There would be a brief presentation of the missionary and his ministry. The host promised anyone who made a financial gift or commitment to this missionary a coupon for a free ride on the yacht at a later date. This event resulted in substantial one-time gifts, and some new regular partners.

The creativity and resources of the advocate are the only limits on the potential of advocacy.

Prayer/Advisory Council

Establishing a Prayer/Advisory Council (PAC) is another way to open the door of ownership. As you look at your list of ten or more primary network members, ask yourself which ones would most likely be able to serve on a PAC.

You are probably wondering just what a PAC is? It is a small group of people (6 to 12) with whom you will meet on a regular basis: once a week, every two weeks, or once a month. It is a subset of your primary network. Because you want to meet with them, at least in the early stages of the PAC, it is necessary for each person to be geographically close: probably within about thirty minutes of a central location.

Geography, of necessity, is a determining factor in whom is selected from your Primary Network to be on the PAC.

Because it is a prayer and advisory group, you will want people on the committee who want to pray for you, and who have gifts like discernment, wisdom, and knowledge. They don't all have to have these spiritual interests or gifts, but these interests and gifts need to be present in some members. Above all, members of the PAC need to be enthusiastic about you and the ministry God is leading you to.

Because the PAC is made up of members of your primary network, most, if not all, of the PAC will be advocates too.

Go back to your list of ten and describe which ones are candidates for your PAC.

Be cautious about inviting strong leadership-type people unless they also know how to function well within a small group; that is, without dominating the group. Couples usually work well in these small groups.

Family members can work well, but caution needs to be exercised. These are family members who are able to put aside strong personal feelings. Remember this group is going to advise you. The group's advice may not always be what you want to hear. For example, they may want you to write a different kind of newsletter. There could be constructive criticism.

Make sure family members on the committee understand the rules of the road and are willing to participate fully without attempting to control. Make sure they can participate without getting defensive regarding their dear son or daughter so that the group does not dysfunction.

Regarding your pastor, here is what to do.

Regarding your pastor, he does not need another group to attend. Here's what to do. Ask to be on his regular schedule. Ask for 15 minutes each week or every two weeks. Allow him to exercise his wisdom, experience, and pastoral role as you share the blessings and challenges of being a missionary. Ask him to pray for you each time you get together. Someone other than the senior pastor (another leadership person in the church) can fulfill this role.

Here's how to start a PAC. Write a letter like the following to those you want to invite to be a member of your prayer/advisory council.

(Sample of PAC letter)

Dear Bill and Bonnie,

Your encouraging note meant a lot to me. And it hasn't been the first time in the last few months that you made me glad God brought you into my life. This thing of being a missionary has presented some challenges, and your prayers and encouragement are a big part in my staying on course.

In fact, you are one of the reasons that I've decided to ask a few of my close friends, and a couple of family members, to consider joining me on a regular basis to pray for me and to advise me.

I'm planning a get together at my house for Saturday evening, April 14, at 6:30. For this first meeting I'm ordering some pizza and salads, and there will be some cold drinks. I'm making a dessert that I know you like. There will be about ten people.

We will discuss the purpose of a prayer/advisory council, how often we might meet, and I will share some of the challenges that I'm facing right now. The council will have an opportunity to discuss these issues with me, and we'll have a time of prayer.

Coming to the first meeting does not obligate you to continue on the council. But it will give you an opportunity to get acquainted and to get a feel for how it will work.

I'll call you in a few days to see if you will be able to make it to the first meeting.

Love,

Jared

One of the outcomes of doing these kinds of activities is that a plan of action begins to take shape.

You have done some serious analysis of your level of trust and value with your primary network, at least ten people. You have evaluated to the point of deciding how each member of your primary network might fit into the activities of advocacy and the prayer/advisory committee. Let's look at another area of analysis: written communication.

When was the last time you wrote this person a personal note or letter? Do you wonder why you are evalating communication? It goes back to the fundamentals: relationship (trust) and service (value). Veteran missionaries know written communication is their lifeline.

As you go down the list of your primary network, think about the last time you wrote these persons a note or letter. You are once again taking a look at your history of relationship building and service.

If you are not a note writer, you need to become one.

If you are not a note and letter writer, you need to become one. (See Chapter Nine for ideas for note writing.)

Notes and letters are an excellent way to serve your friends. It will also become, if it isn't already, the primary means you will have of building, strengthening, and maintaining relationships. It will be the one consistent way you will have, over your career as a missionary, to share your affection and your appreciation.

Start a program of writing personal notes to those whose friendship is important to you, apart from whether they become partners or not.

Missionary life, almost by definition, removes the missionary from personal contact (except for furloughs) with friends and churches at home. Written communication bridges the gap.

You may find that electronic mail will become an effective way to maintain this vital lifeline with some of your network. But please read the chapter about written communication before making electronic mail your total investment in communication.

A successful couple who graduated from a major university

donated six million dollars to their alma mater. When asked, "Why did you give so much money (at that time it was the largest single gift that university had ever received) to this university?" Their simple answer, "Because they asked."

Now be sure to give members of your primary network an opportunity to be an investing partner.

Ownership is the key concept of this chapter, but people who are in your primary network should be given first an opportunity to invest before being asked to take ownership.

Depending upon which mission agency you serve with, the way you handle this particular aspect—presenting the opportunity to be a partner—will be determined by organizational policy. For example, an agency may have the policy: *You must be asked before you can offer an opportunity to financial partnership.* The missionary would, then, have to wait until the friend took the initiative and asked.

If you have the freedom to take the initiative, and trust and value are established, give them or mail your prayer card with a response form. Ask them to pray about being your partner (prayer or financial). Tell them that you will check with them later, or they can mail the response card to you, or to your organization, whichever is appropriate.

Don't do what is suggested in the previous paragraph until you are reasonably sure you have established trust and demonstrated value. People invest in those they trust and value.

Remember the Holy Spirit is superintending the process and He will guide you and give you the freedom and the courage you need. He may also say "No" at times.

But if you are relatively sure of trust and value, give people the opportunity to become a partner. If someone tells you they are thinking and praying about it, be sure to take the initiative to call or write a follow-up note at an appropriate time (use your good judgment). And be praying with them about this decision.

You just finished a healthy exercise. Maybe you see some areas where you need to take some action.

Has the question of motive come to your mind?

Has the question of motive come to your mind? Have you been wondering how a person can know if he isn't just using people to achieve his own goals? Let's take relationships, for example. How would you know if you aren't just building relationships to get partners? There probably is no way to know the answer to that question for sure, but try this.

If you can say to yourself, "It's OK if that person never becomes my partner. My desire to build a personal relationship is because he/she is a person worth knowing, someone I want to know." Then you can have confidence in your motives.

If your service to people and to churches is with no strings attached, then your motives are clear in that dimension.

Most veteran missionaries will say something like this: "Some of the people I expected to support me never did and people I never dreamed would do so, did get involved." So, you see, you really don't have to worry about who will and who won't. It is in the Lord's hands. Just do your part; the Lord will do His part; and God's people will do their part.

The apostle Paul said, *"But as a matter of fact, it matters very little to me what you, or any man, thinks of me—I don't even value my opinion of myself. For I might be quite ignorant of any fault in myself—but that doesn't justify me before God. My only true judge is the Lord"* (1 Corinthians 4:3–4, Phillips).

It isn't that motives are unimportant in relationships and actions, but the apostle also recognized there is a point at which we have to leave the issue of our motives to God.

Remember Peter's admonition: *"Simply concentrate on being completely devoted to Christ in your hearts"* (1 Peter 3:14, Phillips).

Remember this, too, you are a laborer worthy of your hire. You are providing God's people with the opportunity to invest with you in the greatest task and goal presented to the church, going into all the world and preaching the Gospel to every creature. You are inviting people and churches to join you in reaching the world, reaching the world together.

Jesus said to lay up for ourselves treasures in heaven. There is no better way to do that than to invest in missions. Giving people and churches the opportunity to invest with you in the missionary enterprise is an honorable and worthy activity.

"Simply concentrate on being completely devoted to Christ...."

Be honest, open, and transparent with your friends. Have no hidden agendas.

Be alert to potential partners. One missionary couple came to the point where they said, "We have exhausted all of our possibilities. We need some new churches to go to. Why can't the agency (their mission agency) provide us with some churches who might support us? That's what we really need."

This couple was at about 60% of full financial support, supplied by a sending team made up of two churches and about 30 individuals and families.

In an interview with a member of the agency's personnel department, the couple was asked, "How many people and churches are on your mailing list?" Answer: "Oh, we have about 400." Their answer generated this question, "Why do you think you need more contacts when you already have 400 people and churches on your mailing list?"

In the subsequent interview the topics of developing better relationships (trust) with the remaining 370 people and churches in their network, and demonstrating a ministry of service (value) to this segment of their network was thoroughly discussed.

This story points out that there may be another group of people with whom you need to do some evaluation. These are the people and churches with which you are acquainted, but strong personal relationships are lacking. You may not have had time or opportunity to serve them either. This is your General Mailing List, in contrast to your Primary Network.

Veteran missionaries often have 100, 200, 300, and even more of this category of person receiving their newsletters. They are often people with whom the missionary is not well acquainted.

It can happen like this: A clipboard gets passed around in a Sunday school class and members of the class are invited to put their name and address down if they want to be on the guest missionary's mailing list. It often happens that people the missionary does not know very well sign up for the missionary's newsletter.

No matter how the names are added, they can be just names unless the missionary takes initiative to build the relationship and seek opportunities to be a servant to these people.

Make a list of all of the people you have some contact with but who are not in your primary network. Evaluate them in the same manner as you did your primary network.

Make the assumption that people who are not in your primary network are not ready for involvement.

The idea is to start with the very basics with this group of people. Build a foundation of personal relationships and service. Some of these new friends will move over to your primary network as you take the initiative to build trust and demonstrate value and allow the process of selection to be at work.

They are not on the mission field today.

Let's go back to the couple with whom we started this discussion about General Mailing Lists. You may be surprised to know that they are not on the mission field today.

The reason: they refused to take the initiative to build trust and value with some of the 370 additional people and churches who were already at some level of interest and contact. In their belief system, it was God's responsibility to provide them with partners. Have you heard that before? To take action was something they wouldn't do. It was an act of their will, driven by their belief system.

God didn't provide the partners. The mission organization

couldn't provide new churches. The couple wouldn't add action to their faith; they didn't go.

What God had provided was 370 contacts in addition to their primary network (through whom they already had 60% of their support). This is why it is called partnership development.

God does expect us to do our part. Partners are not going to fall off the trees. There is no partner gold mine just waiting for us to discover. Partnership development is not a treasure hunt where you turn up the right rocks and there they are!

There is no partner gold mine just waiting for your discovery.

Are you hearing the ring of truth? Did you know partnership development could involve this kind of work? Let's, as they say in sports, do a "gut check."

Did you complete an evaluation of your Primary Network?

Did you complete an evaluation of your General Mailing List?

Will you?

When?

Set a date for completion _____.

You are probably ready for a break from all the evaluation and detail.

In the next chapter we are going to take another look at the concept of partnership and some associated ideas.

Did you know Jesus is one of your partners?

CHAPTER SEVEN

Getting Clear on the Concepts

Jesus said wise men build on rock (Matthew 7:24). What is the ROCK, the foundations of partnership development?

If Jesus' original message about building on rock had been spoken to the Folopa people of Papua New Guinea there would have been instant understanding.

The Folopa know the importance of understanding issues, concepts, and the basic fundamentals of all life from the ground up. In our culture we often use terms like "bottom line," or "grass roots," attempting to express fundamental issues. The Folopa have a more profound term for it: *Bete'*.

Let's listen as the authors of the book *In Search of the Source* explain the Folopas' concept of the bottom line [The following quote was slightly adapted by this author].

The Folopa are people of the earth. They live at ground level, close to the dirt, out of the soil. The creeping things are their meat. It's straight from the forest to the fire—no middle man. The ground sends up food to fill their bellies; when it goes lean, they do too.

It should be no surprise then that the preeminence of things basic, of root issues, would be ever present in the Folopa mind. It's natural, like the body's need for water.

The term in Folopa is Bete'. It is the fundamental verb of "being" and the most basic metaphor in the entire language.

When Folopas begin to clear undergrowth for a new garden, the biggest part of the work is cutting down and clearing away the trees. But there's something they know about all this process: cutting down a tree does not kill it. Like weeds they keep coming back. A season later new shoots will be up, sprouting at one side or the other out of the trunk. A force below the ground has determined again to reach for the sky.

That, they know, is where the life is. The top part, the part that shows, the part that one can point at and call tree, that's not where the life is. The life is at the base, in the bole, under the ground where you can't see. The Folopa know that if you haven't dealt with that, you haven't dealt with the real issue.

To know Bete' is being on the road to wisdom, to have Bete' can be a goal in life. It can become a quest. People want to know what is out there that will last. What is self-propagating, inexhaustible, ultimate? And how do we tie into it?

As in any society, among the Folopa there is a tyranny of false Bete's. Futureless hopes. Incorrect assumptions. Myths with confused morals. All these tend to undermine and counter honest attempts at grasping reality. If the basis is wrong, how can good grow from it? [1]

If the basis is wrong, how can any good come from it?

Does the partnership model point the way to Bete'? Are the principles **trust, value** and **engaged** self-propagating, inexhaustible, ultimate? Are we on the road to wisdom?

Prospective missionaries, and even some veteran missionaries, are not always sure if they are on the road to wisdom when it comes to partnership development.

Uncertainty is often revealed through questions such as "What's it like to live by faith?" "How is God going to meet my needs?" Or, "How will I get the support I need?" The veteran might ask, "How are we going to double our support as we move from an overseas assignment to a home country assignment?" "Why don't my wife and I agree on this?"

These are some of the questions, but what are the answers?

Because the answers are so important, it is necessary to go a little deeper into the meaning of the principles.

The answers are wrapped up in five concepts—concepts that are so foundational (so Bete') they are worth a chapter all their own. The first is the concept of **partnership**.

CONCEPT 1: PARTNERSHIP

A few years ago I looked up the word "partner" in a Webster's dictionary. I discovered its origin was in the realm of the old wooden sailing ships; which makes sense if we think of the compound word *partnership*.

The old wooden sailing ships had tall masts extending down through each deck level. At each deck level, there were strong timbers wedged around the masts. These timbers supported the masts as each mast bore the stresses and strains of full sails, strong winds, and unpredictable seas.

These strong timbers were called *"partners."*

Now we know why it's appropriate and meaningful to call a missionary's friends and churches partners. We now know why the missionary's network of supporters can be called a partnership.

A missionary's partners are strong timber in his life. It's the prayers, gifts, and encouragements that help the missionary make progress in the midst of his personal and ministry blessings and challenges. Every missionary wants to have his spiritual sails filled with the Holy Spirit, and to make spiritual progress in his own life and encourage progress in the lives of those to whom he is sent.

So, partnership is not just a contemporary business concept. It's not just a ship-building term either. It's also a biblical concept.

The Greek noun *koinonia* is translated in different ways. In Philippians 4:15 Paul describes how the Philippians partnered with him. So partnership is a powerful spiritual term. The same root word, *koinonia,* is translated in other contexts as *communicate, contribute, distribute, fellowship, and partake.* The underlying meaning behind all these definitions is **mutuality.**

The underlying meaning is mutuality.

As with Paul and the Philippians, missions is a ministry of the mutually committed.

In *Final Frontiers,* a thirteen-week mission curriculum for churches by Gospel Light Publications, five aspects of partnership, taken from Philippians, are described: Prayer—Love—Unity—Personal Contact—Finances.[2]

Partnership in Prayer: by the missionary for the senders at home, as well as by the senders for the missionary and their mutual ministry on the field.

Partnership in Love: places senders and the sent on a level with one another, eliminating any saint-on-a-pedestal attitude. Mutual love builds relationships leading to partnership.

Partnership in Unity: having a part as a partner, builds an attitude of ownership, a joint venture mode of thinking. This leads to unity in purpose, or mutual vision.

Partnership through Personal Contact: partners develop attitudes of commitment and responsibility, making them eager to keep in touch. This leads the missionary to make a well-thought-out plan for written communications and personal visits. Close personal contact is difficult to maintain from both sides, but a mutual commitment is made to bridge the gap whenever and however possible.

Partnership in Finances: the Lord supplies funds through financial partners at home. The missionary is mutually responsible for stewardship of finances. Mutual responsibility assures accountability in both directions.

Partnership best describes mutually committed Christians contributing what God gives each of them to reach a common goal.

Partnership is mutually committed Christians contributing to a common goal.

And what has God given? To the missionary it's gifts, experiences and desires leading to a missionary ministry. To the folks at home it's also gifts, experiences and desires—leading to commitment to the five aspects of partnership listed above. And what is the goal? Why does the partnership exist?

PARTNERS WITH A PURPOSE

The body of Christ, the church, is a dynamic, living organism. The Spirit of God leads and empowers it thrusting it out upon the world. The U.S. Center for World Missions reported an incredible statistic in its March 1989 issue of *Mission Frontiers* that shows the dramatic effect of the church's witness. [3]

In the year A.D. 100 there were approximately 360 non-believers for every one believer. Today, there are approximately seven nonbelievers, worldwide, for every believer. Missiologists predicted a ratio of 4 to 1 by A.D. 2000! From 360 to 1; 7 to 1; 4 to 1: we cannot doubt the advancement.

Why do we see such progress? Because...

God is a missionary God.

God is a missionary God. He has declared himself to be a missionary God in two strategic places in the biblical record. In God's covenant with Abraham (Genesis 12:1–4), God said, *"By you all the families of the earth will be blessed."* Every nation, every people group on earth would be blessed through Abraham and his seed (Christ). Israel was to be a witness, missionaries to their neighbors and to the whole world.

When Jesus spoke His Great Commission to the disciples, "Go *and make disciples of all nations"*(Matthew 28:19), He was reiterating the same missionary purpose revealed to Abraham. God was a missionary God in the Old Testament. His overriding purpose for the church of the New Testament is missions.

In Acts 1:8, the church is newly commissioned to God's great purpose. *"But you will receive power when the Holy Spirit comes on you; and you will be my witnesses in Jerusalem and in all Judea and Samaria, and to the ends of the earth."* Those who believe and begin walking in the Spirit, in the light of His Word, are quickly drawn to this purpose. A predominant reason for giving the Holy Spirit and His power to the church was to fulfill the Great Commission.

Therefore, the missionary who goes and the believers who send are **partners with a purpose**. Mutually committed to the purpose of and in tune with the heartbeat of their missionary God: taking the Gospel to the ends of the earth.

WHO ARE THE PARTNERS?

It may seem like this question was already answered. But let's take a look at the answer from a broader perspective. We want to be sure we're clear on the concept. To get as close as we can to that ideal will take more discussion.

The Principle Partner—The Lord Jesus: when Jesus commanded the Great Commission, he made it clear he was a partner in its fulfillment. He said, *"Lo, I am with you always."* We trust we're not in any way reducing his Lordship by calling him a partner. He is both the principle (source of origin) partner and the principal (highest in rank and importance) partner. And He has given us:

The Partner With Power—The Holy Spirit: Jesus told the disciples to *"stay in the city until you are clothed with power on high"* (Luke 24:49). And, *"But you shall receive power when the Holy Spirit has come upon you, and you shall be my witnesses..."* (Acts 1:8). The power of the partnership is not money or even people, it's the Holy Spirit.

The Empowered Partner—The Church: who was it the Lord Jesus told to *wait?* Who was it the Holy Spirit was going to empower? Taken in the context of Acts, chapter one, His power came upon the church to enable it to fulfill the mission-

The power of the partnership is not money or even people; it's the Holy Spirit.

ary purpose of the Godhead —"*You shall be my witnesses...to the ends of the earth.*"

The church is to judiciously use the power given it through the working of the Holy Spirit to accomplish the missionary purpose of God. That is what the book of Acts is all about. It is the church in its individual, congregational, and universal sense.

The church is made up of individual Christians in whom the Holy Spirit resides. "*Don't you know that you yourselves are God's temple and that God's Spirit lives in you*" (1 Corinthians 3:16). The power of the Holy Spirit is worked out, primarily, through obedient individuals, most often banded together in a common cause.

The Instrumental Partner—The Mission Agency: over the years, as the church managed the Lord's mandate, a new phenomenon called a missionary society was born. Mission societies were forerunners of modern-day mission agencies. Missions agencies, both denominational and independent, are now fixtures in the worldwide missionary enterprise.

Even though the focus in this book is on independent faith missions, the word agency includes all expressions of the missionary enterprise, whether denominational, independent faith missions, or churches operating as their own agency.

This phenomenon, the society/agency is a direct result of the Holy Spirit's gifting the church and empowering it to accelerate towards the fulfillment of the Godhead's missionary purpose.

In 1 Corinthians 12:4–6, we're told the gifts given to the church have a varied application in the church and out to the world through the church. "*Now there are varieties of gifts, but the same Spirit; and there are varieties of service, 'different distributions of various kinds of ministries' [Wuest]: but the same Lord; and there are varieties of working, but it is the same God who inspires them all in all.*"[5]

The organized church and the mission agency are intrinsically linked through the power and gifting of the Holy Spirit, and purposes of the Godhead. The church and the agency are by spiritual nature, interactive and interdependent. They are together, the visible, partners! In a real sense, the church is the agency. And the mission agency is **the key instrument** in the hands of the church as it fulfills its missionary mandate. Perhaps it seems strange to say missions agencies are an "instrument in the hands of the church," but this is the correct understanding.

The mission agency is an instrument in the hands of the church.

The Partner Who Acts As Catalyst—The Missionary. Historically, as God worked out the missionary purpose of the church, individual Christians responding to God, acted as catalysts. A catalyst accelerates change. The organized church at large didn't always change immediately. William Carey's vision for India and the rejection of his own church of that vision, is well known. But **the church usually responds to the catalyst whose talk, enthusiasm and energy causes others to become enthusiastic.**

Every missionary acts as the catalyst with a set of individuals and churches who pray, give and encourage—sending and sustaining that missionary. It is the catalyst, causing the vision to be embraced and a partnership to be formed. But the catalyst cannot select himself, or send himself.

In Proverbs 30:22 (KJV) we are told, *"The earth is disquieted by four things, one of which is the servant when he reigneth."* Missionaries are servants. Missionaries should maintain an attitude of humility and submission in the selection and sending process.

CONCEPT 2: MINISTRY IN TWO DIMENSIONS

Ministry is using, under the leadership and power of the Holy Spirit, our spiritual gifts, skills and resources in the service of others.

Wycliffe Bible Translators, a large, reputable mission agency, organized itself around some fundamental principles. One of those principles was "service to all." William Cameron Townsend, the founder of Wycliffe, claimed that it was service to the Cakchiquels of Guatemala and then the Aztecs of Tetelcingo, Mexico that attracted national leaders to his Bible translation ministry. An event from the life of Townsend illustrates this important concept.

While working among the Aztecs of Mexico, the president of Mexico unexpectedly came to visit Cameron and Elvira Townsend. After President Cardenas visited with the villagers and inspected some of the practical projects Townsend helped to get started, they had this interchange, as recorded in the book *Uncle Cam.*[6]

Service to all.
As they walked through the garden, Cam presented his hope of bringing young people to Mexico to translate the Bible into Indian languages. Cardenas shaded his eyes against the hot sun and squinted at the rows of vegetables. 'Will they help the Indians in the practical way you are doing?" he asked.

"Certainly, Señor Presidente," Cam declared. "We only want to follow the example of our Master who came not to be served, but to serve and to give His life for others."

"This is just what my country needs," was Cardenas' response. "Bring all you can get."

That's service in one dimension—on the field. Every missionary needs to realize it's this very same attitude—in another dimension—that makes the difference here at home as the partnership of God's people is sought.

Out of necessity, the spotlight is on the catalyst. Prospective and veteran missionaries need to understand their role as catalyst in the process God employs to bring about and sustain the partnership of individuals, families and churches in the missionary enterprise. On the most basic level, a partnership of the

mutually committed is entered into between a missionary and
that missionary's friends.

Friends are people who share common interests. For Christian friends, the deepest and most enduring interests are
spiritual: interests involving the love of God and the love of
man. It's here, from this arena of spiritual interaction among
friends that we begin to identify prayer partners, financial partners, and encouragers.

If we were to closely examine any group of authentic Christian friends we would see a spiritual dynamic. We would see
God at work among them. The way God works, and how we
see His work, is through the mutual ministry of each to the
other, building one another up in the faith and sharing the Gospel with others. We often hear this spiritual interaction called
ministering.

This is service in that other dimension—at home.

Missionaries serve the body of Christ at home first, and then
serve on behalf of the body of Christ on the mission field. Leaving for the field does not end the responsibility for serving those
at home. Thus, every missionary, whether at home or on the
field, has the wonderful privilege of **ministering in two** dimen-
sions.

A two-dimensional ministry is the key to seeing the Lord
provide the prayer and financial partners the missionary needs
for service on the mission field. Demonstrating spiritual service
at home builds confidence and credibility in that arena. Missionaries serve the church by helping accomplish the purposes
of a local congregation. That may mean in any role for which
they are asked to serve: visitation, teaching, youth work, sweeping the floors, driving the church bus, etc.

Through service, friends and church leaders see the prospective missionary as a loving, committed person with the necessary moral/spiritual maturity and the necessary gifts and skills

Bring all you can get!

to be successful in the missionary enterprise. When the servant gets a vision for missionary service, Christian friends and church leaders catch the vision of the potential ministry out on the field, as an extension of the church. They want to be part of it— partners.

It takes time to serve!

It takes **time** to serve! Mission policies in some churches require a minimum of two years or more of service in the church before a sending commitment can be made by the church. And how long does it take to build a friendship? Sometimes friendships come quickly, but not always.

Scriptural models indicate that God's priorities for ministry at the individual level at home are at least as high as those for ministry in the "uttermost part."

One missionary learned this important truth from an acquaintance while working on their support. It went like this...

Missionary wife: "I'm sure anxious to finish partnership development and get going in our ministry."

Acquaintance: "Mary Anne, you two are doing your ministry—right now!"

Missionary couple's conclusion: "When we realized partnership development was ministry, not getting support (The Lord's job that He does quite well) the burden was off of us and we could minister."

Failure to serve at home under the leadership of a local congregation has caused some missionaries to be unable to develop the necessary partnership team. Also, some missionaries fail to understand that even when they leave for the field they have the privilege and responsibility to minister to those back home through their written communications. It takes priority time, but failure to effectively communicate can mean the erosion of already established relationships and partnerships.

CONCEPT 3: PARTNERSHIP DEVELOPMENT

Within missions over the years, different concepts were used when discussing the challenge of raising financial support. For a long time missionaries called it *deputation*. Then, a more specific term, *raising support*, began to be used. In some circles the term *support discovery* became popular. However, none of these terms captured the most important aspects of the sending process.

For one thing, there was an emphasis on *getting* support and not on service or ministry. You know from reading Concept 2 that getting, as in "Let's go out and get our support," can be an unhealthy and ineffective attitude. It's *giving* in the service of others that's most important.

Go to give, not to get!

The partnership concept was also missing from these earlier expressions. There tended to be the feeling missionaries were acting all alone in their support-raising activities. Missionaries felt alone. That's one reason many missionaries dreaded deputation and raising support.

Support discovery placed emphasis on going out to discover the supporters God had already ordained to give to them. This emphasis seemed to make it more acceptable to faith missionaries. After all, God already has it all worked out, doesn't He?

The trouble is, God doesn't have it laid out like a treasure hunt, as the term support discovery seems to imply. God plans for lives to be touched—needs to be met—the demonstration of ministry—the demonstration of value.

The term partnership development describes the true nature of the sending process. Partnership implies the sending process involves joint ownership. It dispels the notion the missionary is an independent agent. Most missionaries don't like the feelings associated with being independent, anyway. Partnership implies, "Hey, we're in this together."

The concept of partnership strengthens the role of the folks at home. They aren't just praying and giving. They can see the true nature of their involvement as an investor, perhaps even feeling a strong sense of ownership of the missionary's ministry. They have a stake in the outcomes. They can expect accountability. There are and will be mutual rewards.

Partnership development is not a treasure hunt!

The word development emphasizes action on the part of the missionary. The missionary is ministering at home—in person—until going to the field, and by letters, e-mail, telephone, etc. while away. Through active service relationships are built, confidence and credibility established. The missionary isn't just discovering something God has already done, but is actively engaged with the Holy Spirit and other believers in developing relationships from which the sending process can take shape. The missionary is responsible and accountable to God, and to fellow believers, in working out a partnership of mutual commitment within scriptural parameters.

CONCEPT 4: THE LABORER IS WORTHY OF HIS HIRE

The practice of exploiting self-sacrifice, "with the added bromide that employees are involved in a work of love...is evil and despicable."[7]

Jesus was the first one to say it, *"The laborer is worthy of his hire* (Luke 10:7, KJV). The context was when the seventy were sent out two by two. The apostle Paul picked up on this truth in 1 Timothy 5:18, *For the Scripture saith, Thou shalt not muzzle the ox that treadeth out the grain; and, The laborer is worthy of his reward"* (KJV).

The apostle was referring directly to the obligation of the local church to pay the elders that rule well...especially they who labor in the Word and doctrine (verse 17).

The general truth—the laborer is worthy of his hire—is universally accepted in every arena of work. Employers in any society pay employees for their work. The laborer is worthy.

Note this, it is labor that is being paid for, not faith. Jesus and Paul made it clear that it was the laborer who was worthy. Neither Jesus or Paul brought into the discussion an issue such as faith as the medium of exchange. The body of Christ cannot pay its laborers—its elders/pastors/missionaries—or any other worker on the basis of anything other than for their labor. Churches don't pay on the basis of how much faith the pastor, custodian, secretary, or minister of music has.

Faith alone is insufficient.

What are some possible conclusions of the faith missionary who doesn't receive adequate income, and who believes it all rests upon faith?

- God likes that other missionary more than me.
- I don't have enough faith.
- I've committed a sin, and God is withholding my wage.
- I'm sure working hard in my ministry. It doesn't seem fair to work so hard and to be financially short all of the time.
- God is unfair. He isn't holding up His end of the bargain.
- I like being a martyr. I'm proud of living this way. I'm really committed. The people at home see my commitment, and treat me with respect.

Although Michael C. Griffiths in his discussion of the volunteer system does not address this particular downside of being a volunteer, people seen as volunteers may also be seen as persons who forfeit a wage.[8]

Identifying oneself as a volunteer (by selecting oneself) is a dangerous action for most missionaries. Thoughts or statements like "I'm called, I'm going by faith, or I'll call on enough people that I will get enough support" strongly contribute to the perception this missionary is a volunteer.

In the general case, volunteers are not paid. Missionaries who adopt, knowingly or unknowingly, the identity of the volunteer, are undermining their worthiness.

Volunteerism undermines worth.

There is another facet of volunteerism becoming more and more a factor in missionary circles. This is the person or couple who retired from their regular work and want to serve God in missions. These folks come with built-in support, their retirement income.

Self-supported volunteers should be required by church and agency to go through the process of selection, and go to their missionary assignment with a network of spiritual strength standing with them. It's good they can use their own financial resources for support, but having the money to support themselves doesn't qualify them to be missionaries and could leave them without adequate spiritual strength.

The selected laborer is worthy. His labor is worthy of a wage. Missionaries must believe in their worth, their worth of an adequate salary. They must not base financial well being upon a false premise, such as faith alone, or upon their individual sense of call.

CONCEPT 5: WHAT DOES IT REALLY MEAN TO LIVE BY FAITH?

In Galatians, Paul brings together three important truths that point out what it takes to succeed in any aspect of living the Christian life. *"For [if we are] in Christ Jesus, neither circumcision nor uncircumcision counts for anything, but only faith activated and energized and expressed and working through love"* (Galatians 5:6, Amplified New Testament).

Paul points out in this statement three spiritual elements necessary to live the Christian life. **Faith** is identified. Energy, expression, and work are identified. **Action** is a good summary word. **Love** is identified. It takes all three: Faith, Action, and Love.

Faith without action is dead.

Most everyone has ridden a bicycle. Everyone knows it normally takes both legs. If we pedal more with one leg than the other we will be able to ride, but not in a smooth manner. We would tire sooner and enjoy the ride less than when pedaling with both legs.

Riding uphill puts the one-legged rider to the real test. In fact when the going gets tough, the one-legged rider may be in danger of dropping out.

It takes both faith and action to be successful in building a partnership team.

And love, the well-greased chain, transfers the power of faith and action. In 1 Corinthians 13 we are reminded *"Though I have all faith, so that I could remove mountains, and have no love, I am nothing. And though I bestow all my goods to feed the poor [action], and though I give my body to be burned [more action] and have not love, it profiteth me nothing"* (1 Corinthians 13:2–3, KJV).

Faith without love is empty.

The pedals and chain (faith, action and love) move the wheels of the bicycle. The wheels (analogously) transport the missionary through the many activities of partnership development: building relationships with individuals and churches, and serving.

A bicyclist needs nourishment. As the missionary travels down the path of partnership development, he encounters times of fear, frustration, lack of energy to keep going, lack of answers to unexpected situations, etc. It is the Word of God, in a personal sense—a Word from God—that keeps the missionary on track and moving ahead.

There is no time in the missionary's life when a personal relationship with the Lord is more necessary. There is no time when it is more important to be operating by the *promises* and *principles* of Scripture.

Lest it be misunderstood about **promises** and **principles** an explanation, and clarification will be helpful.

Remember when Jesus was tempted by the devil? It is recorded in the gospel of Matthew. The devil came to test Jesus

There is no time in a missionary's life when a personal relationship with the LORD is more important.

after forty days of fasting and praying. The second test was when "*the devil taketh him up into the holy city and setteth him on a pinnacle of the temple, and saith unto him, 'If thou be the Son of God, cast thyself down; for it is written, He shall give his angels charge concerning thee, and in their hands they shall bear thee up, lest at any time thou dash thy foot against a stone.' Jesus said to him, 'It is written again, Thou shalt not put the Lord, thy God, to the test'*" (Matthew 4:5–7, KJV).

The devil quoted a promise right out of the Old Testament in his attempt to trick Jesus into compliance. Even though the test was presented in terms of a legitimate promise, Jesus rejected that promise in this situation. Jesus brought forth a principle that governed and guided the application of the quoted promise, and consequently prevented him from a disastrous decision.

What is the application to partnership development? When one is claiming promises, be sure to understand the principles that guide and govern the outworking of that promise.

Promise + Principle = Harmony with God and man

Promise − Principle = Presumption/Disharmony

Claiming promises without understanding the context and guiding principles is shaky ground.

Claiming promises without understanding the context and the guiding principles is shaky ground for any believer. Missionaries should not base their partnership development activities upon promises alone.

Faith without action [scripturally endorsed and socially appropriate action] is anti-faith: demonstrates no value—profits nothing.

Faith without love has no pleasant melody—has no ring of truth and undermines trust.

PERSONAL APPLICATION

How can I apply the five principles of Partnership in my ministry, now?

a. Prayer —

b. Love —

c. Unity —

d. Personal Contact —

e. Finances —

These are ways I already serve and minister in the local church.

a.

b.

c.

I see myself taking steps in developing partner relationships by:

a.

b.

c.

etc.

END NOTES

[1] Neil Anderson with Hyatt Moore, *In Search of the Source, A First Encounter With God's Word*, Portland, Oregon, Multnomah Press, 1992, from the chapter Bete': The Source, pp. 43-50.

[2] *The Final Frontier, Exploring God's Plan for World Missions, A Bible Study For Layman*, Sherie Lindvall, Managing Editor, Steven A. Hardy, Writer, Ventura, California, Gospel Light Publications, 1985, *Session Twelve, Aspects of Partnership*.

[3] Mission Frontiers. Bulletin of the U.S. Center for World Mission. Vol. 11, Nr. 3, March 1989. The chart has been updated in subsequent volumes of Mission Frontiers, but the basic profile of progress is the same.

[4] George Cowan, *Bible Translation Since John Wycliffe, In Other Words*, Wycliffe Bible Translators Progress Report, Vol. 10, No. 1, January/February 1984.

[5] Kenneth S. Wuest, *The New Testament: An Expanded Translation*, Grand Rapids, Michigan, William B. Eerdmans Publishing Company, 1968.

[6] James and Marty Hefley, *Uncle Cam*, Milford, Michigan, Mott Media, 1981, p. 94.

[7] Lloyd Billingsly, *To Him that Worketh*, Eternity Magazine, January 1985. The quote within the quote is from Lewis Smedes, Fuller Seminary ethics professor.

[8] Michael C. Griffiths, *Who Really Sends The Missionary*, Chicago, Moody Press, 1972, pp. 12-23.

CHAPTER EIGHT
• • • • • • • • •

Partnership Tools

Some years ago, a farmer inherited an unproductive piece of land. With knowledge, skill, and hard work the farmer slowly turned the property into one of the most beautiful and productive farms in the area. One day the farmer invited his pastor for a visit. As they toured the farm the pastor kept exclaiming at how God had provided such beautiful soil; how God had blessed the man with such tall corn, and beautiful hay fields; and on and on.

Finally the farmer could stand it no more and exclaimed, "You know, pastor, you should have seen it when God was doing it by himself!" The farmer wasn't upset with God, but he was a little miffed that the pastor didn't recognize his part in the productive output of the farm.

"Pastor, you should have seen it when God was doing it by Himself."

Yes, as has been said all along in this book, God expects missionaries to do their part. It is not by faith alone; by action alone; or by love, alone. The farmer applied knowledge, skill, and hard work, to develop the resource God had provided. He also had the right tools.

So far in this book, the emphasis has been on the knowledge, spiritual skill, and hard work required to be successful in the development of a complete partnership team.

It is time to talk about tools. Partnership tools can be

divided into these two categories: audio/visual and print. In this chapter we will discuss some basic print media tools.

What tools are needed to help the missionary be successful in relating to others, and to demonstrate value, and to be engaged? What information and opportunities does the interested church or individual need to become a partner? How does the missionary provide that information and opportunity?

The tools described in this chapter perform more than one function.

FUNCTION 1   **Reinforce the Principles of the Partnership Model**

Partnership tools link the missionary and mission agency to the interested church and individual while trust and value are in process. These tools are an important part of building trust, demonstrating value, and being engaged. Good tools help missionaries build and strengthen relationships. Good tools help missionaries in various ways to serve and to minister, whether in a church or among individuals and families. Partnership tools reinforce the principles of the partnership model.

FUNCTION 2   **Provide Closure**

The second function, then, is to help the interested church and individual, at different times in the process, to come to closure when they desire to enter into partnership. When trust and value are the goal, interested churches and people are the natural outcome, with some of them taking the step of partnership.

The Holy Spirit superintends the process. He will provide the partners when the missionary does his part.

FUNCTION 3   **Help Maintain and Expand the Team**

The third function is to provide the means for maintaining and expanding the partnership team in the years ahead. Even the short-term missionary will want to take the long-range view because many short-termers decide to go career. Transition from short term to career is much easier if the long-range view is taken from the beginning.

What is meant by maintaining? Maintaining, in partnership development, means the missionary sustains continuous activity in writing personal notes and letters, has a regular newsletter program, and plans for as much personal contact as possible. With communications capabilities through fax, telephone, and e-mail, as well as the written letter, missionaries have no excuse for not maintaining regular contact with their constituencies.

Maintenance means the missionary stays in business.

Staying in Business

Business people today spend from 35% to 60% of their time staying in business; not doing business but staying in business.

It is God's people who keep missionaries in business. When God's people withdraw from the support of missionary causes it is possibly due to the missionary's negligence. Negligence in building and maintaining the vital linkage to, and interest of partners may force the missionary out of business.

Missionaries have to work at staying in business.

Maintaining and expanding are both necessities. Maintaining, perhaps, would be expected, but what about expanding?

The Hidden Agenda

A hidden agenda in missionary life has caused some missionaries real difficulties.

Fact: the budget most missionaries start out with is a budget based upon the first year of service.

What about the second year, the third and fourth? This is the hidden agenda. Missionaries who go to their assignments, even with full support, will by the second year be under-supported. Unless missionaries take steps to expand their partnership team, by the third and fourth years there will be a serious gap between budget and income.

It is not unusual for a missionary to experience a 15% to 20% drop in financial partnership over the course of a full term (4 to 5 years) of service, thus creating a serious financial gap between budget and income.

The Gap

What causes the gap? A number of things, but the most obvious are **attrition, inflation, and new expenses** not calculated in the original budget. What may not be so obvious but just as real, is going to a mission assignment without adequate support.

Attrition is the inevitable result of people, perhaps a church, starting out as partners but dropping out. Attrition is to be expected. People lose jobs, churches experience a lag in giving, churches go into building programs and cut back on missions when money gets tight, churches split, and people sometimes become disenchanted with missions. Whatever the reason, attrition is to be expected.

Inflation can take on a number of faces. The reduction of the value of the dollar in another country's economy (rate of exchange) may seriously reduce a missionary's buying power. And the cost of goods and services may go up dramatically apart from the rate of exchange. For example, rent may increase in huge chunks. Change of assignment location within a country may find the missionary paying city costs, instead of village costs that are associated with living in a more rural setting.

New expenses (birth of a child, expansion of ministry, schooling for the children, buying a vehicle, unexpected medical expenses, etc.), can, if not planned for, make financial life very difficult for the missionary.

"Don't leave home without it!" was a powerful byline for American Express. It is an appropriate slogan for missionaries.

Leaving for an assignment without a complete partnership

"Don't leave home without it!"

team, in view of the other gap factors mentioned above, sets the missionary up for financial difficulty. It can even mean failure.

Financial difficulties can lead to friction in relationships, both within a family and within the mission. Financial failure can lead to marital failure, spiritual failure, and failure in the missionary's assignment.

Going to another country, culture, and language to communicate profound spiritual truth and live an exemplary Christian life is challenge enough without having to deal with the consequences of inadequate financial resources.

Let's ask ourselves the question, *Should missionaries be sent to spiritual warfare from a position of weakness, or strength?*

Going to an assignment without being fully armed for the long haul is going in weakness.

Lack of finances is not the only indicator of potential weakness, but it is a well-known reality. Prayer support is closely linked to financial support. Most often those who give are those who pray.

What can the missionary do about this hidden agenda? If it's not possible or practical to raise the money for a budget that encompasses the needs for a full term, instead of just the first year, what can be done?

The only practical, realistic answer is to make sure the agenda is not hidden (not just to the missionary but also to his friends). Missionaries should do the kinds of things discussed in this book; so when expansion of the team is necessary, the foundation is in place from which to expand.

Missionaries must guard against allowing the GAP to grow to crisis proportions. Good partnership tools used at the right times in appropriate ways will keep that from happening.

Partnership development tools are many and varied. The following are some representative examples with some explana-

Missionaries should be sent in strength, not in weakness.

tion of how and when to use them. The focus will be on basic tools frequently used by missionaries.

Partnership Tools

Prayer Card

Missionaries use prayer cards more than any other tool. Most missionaries have enough printed so that everyone on the mailing list can receive one, and have a few left over to hand out at appropriate times.

If developing partners is a major activity (a lot of partners still needed and many opportunities for sharing in churches and meeting with people are ahead) then it is recommend to have at least 100 extra cards. With a mailing list of 200, and adding 100 extra, that's an order of 300.

This is a judgment call. But it's far better to have too many, than to run out. Print shops will keep the original setup work (or return it to the missionary) and will be able to run off additional copies in fairly short notice. With a reorder, there would be opportunity to update information.

Prayer Cards With Response Envelope

When missionaries want to include a response mechanism with a prayer card, they might include a response envelope. Envelopes with a return address, options for involvement pre-printed on the flap and places for the missionary's name and account number and pertinent partner informtion are in common use.

Prayer Card With Attached Response Form

Many prayer cards have a response form attached, often with a perforated edge. But some of these require an additional response envelope to make it convenient for mailing the card back to the missionary, or to the missionary's organization.

Prayer cards are the basic partnership tool for most missionaries because they:

1. Usually are smaller than other types of literature used by missionaries.
2. Require smaller envelopes.
3. Can be magnetized and attached to metal surfaces, like a refrigerator door.
4. Can be bi-fold and stand alone on any flat surface: a person's desk.
5. Function both as a prayer card and financial response tool. When the response card is removed, the picture portion remains as a reminder to pray.
6. Present a wide variety of possibilities in design.
7. Easily and inexpensively personalized.
8. Can have color photos, maps and other design features making attractive literature.
9. Are relatively inexpensive.
10. Reprint easily when reorders are necessary.
11. Are available through several printing companies who specialize in this type of literature. Most mission agencies can provide the names of several companies that print prayer cards. Many mission agencies provide this printing service to their own missionaries.

How are prayer cards used?

Most missionaries send prayer cards along with a regular newsletter. When a prayer card is enclosed in a newsletter, a section of the newsletter should be used to explain why the card has been enclosed. But even if the prayer card is not sent with a newsletter, a cover letter that explains the purpose of the card and provides helpful information should be included.

Missionaries shouldn't assume the reader understands what to do with the card. Missionaries should be aware of any guidelines their organization has regarding mention of financial sup-

Missionaries shouldn't assume that their friends know what to do.

port. But within those guidelines, provide a clear statement of the purpose of the card, and clear instructions on how to use the card.

It is also helpful to the potential partner to know what will happen if the card is sent back to the missionary, or the missionary's organization. If the card goes to the organization, will the missionary be informed? Are tax-deductible receipts issued? Will the person responding be placed on any other mailing lists?

Information Brochure

A slightly more complex piece (and expanded version of the prayer card) is an information brochure. It has all of the elements of a prayer card (photo, addresses, etc.), but more information.

Response pieces are for the benefit of your friendship. Make them as easy to use as possible.

Brochure-type literature is recommended when the missionary is making a lot of new contacts with people who may not know very much about missions, about the missionary's particular mission, or about the partnership basis of prayer and financial support.

Often missionaries need to give their interested friends and churches more than one opportunity to become a partner. Having a prayer card and a brochure-type piece will provide the missionary with some variety in mailings and at presentations.

Newsletter with response form

Newsletters can be designed to include a tear/cutoff response form as a section at the bottom of the letter. This will make a response envelope necessary. This is a simple, inexpensive, straightforward way to encourage prayer and financial partnership.

Never send a response form of any type that does not have included with it an easy means of return. It is really important to make it as easy as possible for the recipient to complete the form and get it in the mail. Put a stamp on the return envelope, or card. Self-addressed, postage-paid return envelopes or cards are the most convenient way to assist partners in their responses. Of course, cost is a factor. Missionaries usually let the partner provide the stamp.

Strategy

Interested friends and churches often need more than one opportunity to come to closure and make the commitment to be a partner. Missionaries who take a lone-range view of partnership will plan to have more than one partnership tool, especially partnership tools that provide for a response. Any missionary engaged in serious partnership development will probably have to plan to provide *at least five opportunities* for response through newsletter mailings alone.

Provide at least five opportunities for response.

A variety of tools like a prayer card with response card attached, a prayer card with response envelope, a brochure with response form, and a newsletter with response form are useful instruments and provide the variety needed.

Some response tools can be used more than once, but variety is a useful tactic.

A business card, although generally not associated with an opportunity to become a partner, is also a useful tool.

Business Card

The business card is handy to give to people with whom you've just established a relationship. Some missionaries hand out business cards at every opportunity: the gas station, grocery store, post office, etc. During these casual encounters, the missionary will usually have an opportunity to say who he is and what he does, and mention that he speaks in churches, schools, and to professional groups. A helpful follow-through could be, "Keep my card handy, if you ever need a speaker, let me know."

Through these kinds of encounters missionaries have had

many opportunities to develop new relationships and to minister in a variety of situations. Some of these opportunities have led to solid personal relationships, and also on to partnership.

Weight

Weight is always a consideration when putting together a mailing. Gather equivalent or actual pieces so that the total can be weighed to determine the postage. Most of the time, a prayer card or brochure can be accompanied by at least a one-page, 8½ by 11 letter and still stay under one ounce.

Information Portfolio

Information portfolios are a special partnership tool. These are not mass produced for mailing to an entire mailing list. Usually 15 to 25 are sufficient. Information portfolios are primarily for pastors, missions committees, prayer/advisory committees (PAC), and advocates. Portfolios provide a handy reference and source of information about the missionary and his mission. Most pastors or missions committees would welcome having this kind of document for reference.

Prayer/advisory committees need this kind of in-depth information and understanding to be adequately informed in prayer and to be able to give good advice. Advocates can use the portfolio to pass on to someone else: a pastor, missions committee, or interested friend.

Depending upon how and with what materials a portfolio is constructed determines how much each will cost, and how labor intensive it will be.

While discussing the idea with his prayer/advisory committee, one missionary found the whole project being taken on by a member of his PAC who happened to be in desktop publishing. All the missionary had to do was to provide the information.

If the pages of information are produced by computer, up-

Portfolios provide:

1. Front cover with photo, name of organization, name of missionary and address, telephone number and e-mail address.

2. Indexed pages that tell:

a. Purpose of mission

b. Missionary's role

c. Missionary's testimony

d. Location of mission

e. Financial profile

f. Different ways the missionary can serve in the church

g. Endorsement letter

h. Use photos, drawings, etc. as much as possible.

dating of information on particular pages is easy if additional portfolios are needed. A portfolio produced with a clear plastic front cover, three-hole folder, purchased from a stationery or office supply store will cost less than $1.00 each. More involved productions with paste-on color photos and specially designed folders can cost as much as $5.00 each.

No matter which kind of production chosen, most missionaries find this to be a good investment. It wasn't until a missionary on furlough, after several previous visits to a church with opportunities to share, sent the pastor a portfolio that real interest developed. The pastor, in fact, mentioned the portfolio as the turning point for him. His attention was attracted to the missionary's ministry in a new way. The church became partners.

Annual Report

Every major organization sends its stockholders a yearly report. Missionaries' partners can be viewed as stockholders.

Annual reports may be incorporated into portfolios.

An annual report is an excellent way to bring a constituency up to date on what has been happening in a ministry: what goals were accomplished, challenges, prayers answered, etc. It is also an opportunity to lay out next year's plans, goals, and prayer requests. One section can be used to report the year's financial profile, both in ministry, and personal needs. Financial needs may be projected for the next year.

How financial matters are reported in an annual report would have to be in line with the policies of the particular organization. Graphs and percentages, and number of partners needed can be used as a way of communicating need. Use dollar amounts when authorized by the mission agency.

Financial Profile

The financial profile may be sensitive for missionaries who belong to a faith mission. Financial profiles by nature contain specific financial information. Some faith missions do not allow their missionaries to state or put in print specific financial information, or to provide such information unless asked.

In spite of possible restrictions, the financial profile is an excellent document to have handy when raising support. Missionaries are often asked by missions committees for specific financial information. Prayer/advisory committees and advocates would want this kind of information. Frequently, in church and home-type meetings, specific questions are asked which would provide the missionary the freedom to hand out a financial profile.

When preparing a financial profile, keep the budget categories general in nature. The missionary doesn't need to provide detailed descriptions of any category of budget.

"Wow, I think I'll become a missionary. You guys make more than I do!"

When answering questions about finances, be aware that most people do not know that missionaries are self-employed. Being self-employed means that the missionary pays all of his expenses, including all of what is often called benefits. For example, the self-employed missionary pays all of Social Security. The person employed by a company or public agency will probably have at least half of the Social Security assessment paid by that employer.

The level of self-employment varies among mission agencies. Some missionaries pay all of their benefits, including life insurance, worker's compensation insurance, health insurance, Social Security, retirement, plus a percentage assessment to the organization.

These various fees, taxes, and assessments can account for 50% of a missionary's monthly budget. This is why the career missionary's budget seems higher than what some people would expect. Some missionaries serving overseas have other factors in their budgets, for example, children's education. This is especially costly if a boarding school is used.

Missionaries need to fully understand their financial profile. It isn't unusual to have someone from an audience say something like this, "Wow, I think I'll become a missionary. You guys make more than I do! " A person saying this would probably be unaware of the self-employed nature of the missionary.

The missionary cannot leave a statement like the above hanging. It must be responded to. Having an in-depth understanding of how one's budget is formed, and being able to explain it without going into too much detail is necessary in these situations.

The self-employment concept can be very helpful in increasing the understanding of an audience, or individual. There are self-employed people in almost every audience who might lend their own experience to the discussion. The missionary might ask if anyone in the audience is self-employed, and thus provide an opportunity for input from others.

Not only is the missionary often in the self-employed category, but his total life and ministry is very much like operating a small business.

Monthly Financial Log

Maintaining a monthly financial log is a simple way to keep track of how God is providing for your needs through financial partnership. The major benefit is to be able to see the pattern of giving of individuals and churches, so that if some irregularity occurs you will know it right away. You will also be aware when someone increases support without making any direct mention of it to you.

If you don't keep any other record, keep this one!

If you don't keep any other kind of partnership records, don't fail to keep this one: the monthly financial log.

Lapsed Partners

When someone has given regularly and suddenly stops without any explanation, it usually means something happened in their life that was unusual, causing them to break the cycle. Review all that you know about this partner to see if there is something you are aware of that could cause this lapse. The history of giving—irregular or regular—is a clue. Sickness, birth of a baby, travel, etc. are possible causes for a lapse.

What to do when someone unexpectedly stops giving.

If you know of no reason why this partner would stop, then do the following.

- Check with the receipts department of your organization to make sure the partner's gift wasn't mistakenly (although rare, it occasionally happens) applied to someone else. If not,

- Ask the receipts department if this person or church gives to any other missionary in your organization; if so, did they give to that other person(s) that month. This will usually reveal that the lapse affected each missionary to whom the partner was giving. If so,

- Allow one additional month so that the partner has a chance to come back in the next month. This often happens.

If the partner hasn't come back in by the second month, then a note or telephone call is probably appropriate. Experience shows that it is most often the right thing to do—to write or call.

One church stopped giving while the pastor was on the mission field visiting the church's missionaries. The financial secretary quit while the pastor was away. The mission committee had no idea that the checks to missionaries were not written for two months. It was summer and the committee wasn't meeting. When informed by a missionary that a check hadn't come for two months, the chairman of the committee was grateful for the information, and the church got back on track quickly. In this particular case, the church supported other missionaries. None of the other missionaries had inquired. The missionary who called had done a service for others, not only for himself.

It is never wrong to communicate. In every case of which

150

this author is aware, the partner has been grateful when told of the lapse. Lapses do occur for very understandable reasons. Some of these reasons are mentioned above.

It is never wrong to write.

There is a tendency for the missionary to think he, the missionary, did something wrong and that is why the partner quit giving. This is rarely the case.

What might a partner think if he discovered his own lapse after two or three months, and realized the missionary had never said anything? It's possible the partner would conclude, *I guess they didn't need it. They never even noticed.*

A brief note is just as appropriate as a telephone call, and may be easy for the partner to receive. It may be easier for the missionary to write than to call.

Enclose a self-addressed, postage-paid postcard with the written note. Ask the partner to let you know if anything unusual has been happening, and to let you know if there is anything about which you can be praying.

Correspondence Log

Correspondence logs are useful for maintaining a complete record of all correspondence with everyone on the mailing list. These types of correspondence logs which are used as records for each person, or family, or church are available from many sources.

Using the Internet and any search vehicle, type in the words "prayer card," or "record keeping." Multiple options will appear for your your perusal.

Computer software is available for this kind of record keeping, as well as for creating one's own systems and forms. Visiting a computer software store, browsing through what they offer, will present you with several options for record keeping.

It may take some trial and error to find the correspondence log that is best for you.

Many missionaries already use these materials. Check with other missionaries if you are uncertain how to proceed.

Third-party letters

Third-party letters are written on behalf of the missionary.

There are two types of third-party letters: letters of endorsement and letters telling about financial need.

Letters of Endorsement

Someone who desires to communicate the following kinds of things to the missionary's constituency writes letters of endorsement.

1. Commends those who are already partners for their commitment, care, and prayer. Expresses how they are already contributing to the missionary enterprise, even if the missionary is still in a training stage.

2 Validates the missionary's role (assignment) along with telling how the missionary is specifically contributing to the spiritual results the mission is achieving. It is also an endorsement of the missionary's Christian character.

   The letter validates the missionary's work and his life. It provides some insight into how this missionary's life impacts his fellow missionaries and the community.

   If the letter is written about a husband and wife, the contribution of both should be referred to, even if the wife is engaged in the ministry of wife and mother. The husband and wife are a team, and should be written about in those terms.

3. Tells something about the overall work of the mission and what the future in terms of expected results looks like. Tells why this missionary is needed in order for these expected results to happen.

Letters of endorsement are valuable even at the beginning of a missionary's career. The mission administrator, to whom the missionary is assigned, could write a letter of endorsement primarily expressing expectations of what it will mean to have this missionary on assignment.

The missionary's pastor could write a letter of endorsement

and recommendation in which the pastor could express the reasons why his/her church is supporting and praying for this missionary. Members of a PAC or an advocate could write a letter of endorsement.

Letters of endorsement can be a page in the information portfolio, described earlier.

Financial Need Letters—A Harvest Tool

Financial need letters are really letters of endorsement with two added elements: an expression of financial need and a response form.

This type of third-party letter will probably be written infrequently, usually at a strategic time in a missionary's partnership development process, or at a time when there is a specific financial crisis: sudden drop in support, heavy medical bills not covered by insurance, etc.

For the entry-level missionary a financial need letter usually works best toward the end of the partnership development process. This type of letter is more a harvest tool than a fund-raiser. It helps the missionary harvest all of the plowing, planting, and cultivating (relationship building and service/ministry) that has been done during the partnership process.

For the entry-level missionary, the best results come when the missionary has had fairly recent (within a year) face-to-face contact with the majority of people on his mailing list, and has maintained a regular program of written communication: newsletters and personal notes.

The letter with response form provides another opportunity for the person who said they would like to be a partner but hasn't yet started. It provides an opportunity to the person who has been praying about it but hasn't made a decision.

This type of third-party letter helps the most when the missionary is somewhere around 75 to 80% of their needed support. The letter provides not only a validation but usually a sense of urgency. The urgency factor—time is getting short—is a powerful incentive. It helps the missionary get over that last hump, but it only helps significantly if the missionary has been doing his part in relationship building, serving, and engaging.

What percentage of the people on your mailing list would know you if they saw you on the street?

How would a missionary know if it is the right time for a financial need letter? The answer to this question—*What percentage of the people on your mailing list would know you if they saw you on the street?*—will be a strong indicator. It doesn't do much good to write a letter asking for financial partnership if the reader can't even remember who this missionary is. It's a harvest tool, not a fund-raiser.

If the missionary maintains a high level of communication with his constituency and has seen most of the people and churches in his network within the past twelve months, a financial need letter should produce a good result.

For new missionaries, beginning with a letter of endorsement, and using the financial need letter toward the end of the partnership process can be a helpful combination.

Missionaries who are coming home on furlough may find that a letter of endorsement from their field supervisor will be helpful. This letter of endorsement should be mailed as close in time as is possible to the missionary's arrival home. It could even precede their arrival home.

If, during their time at home, missionaries find that they need to raise additional support, a third-party financial need letter would be a nice follow up to the letter of endorsement. The financial need letter could be mailed within a month to six weeks after the letter of endorsement. Or the need letter could be kept as a tool to use only if time revealed that this letter was necessary.

Using these kinds of letters is often a judgment call.

Momentum

Imagine a missionary's newsletter. Stick-figure-type images of people form the border starting about halfway down the right side of the front page, proceed across the bottom, and ascend to the top left corner of the page. Intermixed with the images of people are about five box-like drawings with steeples. Those are the five churches that already support the missionary. Adding the number of people to the churches the reader of this newsletter can see the missionary's current partnership team.

The last image at the top left corner where the line of partners ends is that of the missionary. This missionary is holding a flag, or banner. On the banner it says "75%."

At the top on the right side of the page there is a photo representing the missionary's ministry. The photo might be a classroom (if the missionary teaches, or a scene depicting a witnessing event, etc.). Right under the photo is a quote from Scripture that says, "Come over and help us" (Acts 16:9, often referred to as the "Macedonian call").

Now, the space between the missionary holding the banner and the photo representing the place and type of ministry is marked off in increments representing percentages: 80%, 85%, 90%, etc.

This momentum graphic shows a missionary at 75% support with a good network of individual/family/church partners standing with him. He needs the help of his family and friends, and his current partners, to reach his destination—his ministry. The text of the newsletter will explain what is needed to make the momentum image meaningful.

However, the best momentum graphics require the least text. The graphic should bear the weight of communication. The reader should be able to get the picture just from the graphic.

What is the picture? This missionary needs an additional 25% in financial support in order to leave for his assignment.

Or, the increments could be stated in dollar amounts, or in the number of new partners needed.

What is the message to the reader? This missionary is posing two questions to his readership: "Can you help me?" and, "How can you help?" This is where explanatory text fulfills its role as the missionary explains how the reader can help. It's important that the message conveyed has a sense of urgency. "We need a complete partnership team by July 20." Following, then, would be the details of why this date.

I remember one missionary who used sailboats to represent his current level of partnership. He had six small sailboats spaced across the Pacific Ocean from the shores of California to the islands of the Philippines. Each sailboat represented 10% of his support: six sailboats. Obviously he needed four more sailboats to complete his partnership team.

After the missionary's newsletter went out with this graphic and some explanation, he received a telephone call. The lady said, "We were meaning to have some of our friends over and have you come and share. We didn't realize how important it was to do this now, until we got your last letter. If you can come on (a date was given) we will invite some friends for the evening."

Then, she said, "**Maybe we can help you get another sailboat!**"

Her statement meant the purpose of this momentum graphic was realized. The reader saw what was needed, interpreted this need in terms of her resources, and took action. To her this was something doable. The missionary wasn't asking her to raise any particular amount of money. The steps, or increments, represented in this graphic were clear and doable. She didn't have to take on the task of getting four sailboats, just one. And, she saw that it was ok to say, "*Maybe* we can help...."

By the way, after three newsletters containing this sailboat graphic, over the period of about three months, the remaining four sailboats were added. After the first newsletter with the graphic, through actions on the part of friends and family like the lady mentioned above, two sailboats were added.

So, in the second newsletter, there were eight sailboats. In the third newsletter, there were ten sailboats, and the missionaries were scheduling their flight.

The concept of momentum is probably the most difficult partnership development tool to use effectively. Missionaries using this concept should be sure to test it out with an alert friend to make sure the graphic design chosen communicates exactly what is desired. Remember, too, the real test of effectiveness is the reader saying, *"I can help do that!"*

These are the important characteristics of a momentum graphic:

1. It is dynamic. There is a sense of movement and progress.
2. There is tension. That is, the graphic shows an objective that is not yet reached, but is reachable.
3. There are steps—doable steps—that if each is achieved the objective (a complete partnership team) will be achieved.
4. The steps (the number of partners needed, for example) seem doable to the reader. The reader can see himself helping to achieve at least a part of one of the steps.
5. The goal is stated in terms of ministry results. For example, the goal might say, *To take my assignment in Kenya so that I can join the team of evangelists and church planters working in the inner city of Nairobi.*

NOTE, the goal is *not* to get more partners. A complete partnership team is needed, and that is the purpose of the momentum graphic, but it is not the goal. The fulfillment of ministry is the goal. Partners are necessary to the fulfillment of that goal.

The best time to introduce a momentum graphic into a newsletter is after 50–60% of needed partnership is reached.

There needs to be momentum to build momentum. It's possible to use momentum too early in the partnership process. The reader of the newsletter that has a momentum graphic needs to see that God is already blessing, that churches and friends have already joined the partnership team.

Some partners will catch the idea and will say, "I can help do that"—ownership.

Don't expect any tool by itself to produce partners in ministry. The missionary always has to have done the basic relationship building (building trust), and have been serving in as many ways in as many places as possible (demonstrating value). Everything else grows out of these basics.

Remember it is service with no strings attached. The Holy Spirit superintends the process. If you are doing your part, you can count on God to bless you.

"The tools are only as good as the person using them."

There is another reality every missionary has to face: the tools are only as good as the person using them.

The tools assist the missionary under the leadership of the Holy Spirit to bring the process to closure with those whose interest has developed into the desire to be a partner.

Know your tools, have a variety available, develop your skills and understanding in using these tools.

CHAPTER NINE

• • • • • • • • •

The Gift of a Letter

You don't owe anybody a letter. Letters are a gift.
—Garrison Keillor

Written communication is the missionary's lifeline. Most missionaries spend, over their careers, very little time in the presence of their friends, family, and churches. Lines of communication most often pass through the written word.

Some missionaries view writing as drudgery. I understand that completely. That's the way I thought of it until a friend introduced me to the idea that our written communication really is a gift.

Garrison Keillor wrote, *"Such a sweet gift, a piece of handmade writing, in an envelope that is not a bill, sitting in our friend's path when she trudges home from a long day spent among wahoos and savages, a day our words will help repair."*[1]

Have you ever thought of your letters and notes as "sweet gift[s]"?

Now, Keillor isn't talking about formal writing. He is talking about personal notes and letters. Are you reluctant to write personally? Would it make it easier if this kind of communication is thought of as a gift? It did for me.

"So a shy person sits down and writes a letter. To be known by

another person, to meet and talk freely on the page, to be close despite distance. To escape from anonymity and be our own sweet selves and express the music of our souls.[2]

Can you be that kind of person, writer; to be close despite distance? You can. I did.

I've been writing personal notes for about fifteen years. I didn't know if I was connecting with people until one day at Sunday school one of our financial partners, who had received a personal note of appreciation from me, said to my wife, "Thanks for that really nice note, Dona!" Dona responded, "My husband wrote that!"

"My husband wrote that."

Talk about "making my day."

There's another way I know I'm connecting. Since I started writing notes of appreciation to our partners on a regular basis there has been a significant difference in our financial partnership. Dona would confirm this.

Alexandra Stoddard, in her book, *Gift Of A Letter* says, "*When written from the heart, letters are dreams on paper, wishes fulfilled, desires satisfied. Letters can be powerful.*"[3]

"*When I write a letter to a friend, I bring that person into my day, describing domestic events, my mood, my attitude, colors and pleasures. A cut finger, my cold, news of my children, the weather, music, smells from the kitchen, are all shared. If I write a letter late at night in the intimacy of one lamp I tend to describe my surroundings and the stillness. If I write a letter from a restaurant I might describe what looks good on the menu. Scenes are painted, stories told that linger as long as the letter, and beyond.*"[4]

Keillor comments on the longevity of a letter in this way. "*Probably your friend will put your letter away, and it'll be read again a few years from now and it will improve with age. And forty years from now, your friend's grandkids will dig it out of the attic and read it....*"[5]

Robert Louis Stevenson said, "*The difficulty is not to write, but to write what you mean, not to affect the reader, but to affect him precisely as you wish."*[6]

That is a tall order for a missionary, to affect the reader of his correspondence precisely as he wants to. Is this really possible? Can missionaries write with that kind of purpose and force? How?

Most missionaries will not achieve the level of skill of a Robert Louis Stevenson. But can we grow in this skill? Yes, but for the missionary who wants to be a good writer it will be a lifelong goal.

Maybe we need to, first, address the question, does a missionary even need to write to his partners?

Yes, is probably self-evident, but it might help reinforce that answer by reading what one missionary's partner had to say to me about lack of communication.

"We first met them about seven or eight years ago when we volunteered at their mission's office. We were impressed with their sincerity and their seeking the Lord's will for their lives. We started supporting them. It's been over a year since we heard from them. Their communication has been sporadic at best and often non-existent. This is a great contrast to the other missionaries we have supported in the past who regularly write to us and encourage us as to the workings of the Lord in the field. Such communication strengthens our own faith and lets us know that our support is needed and put to good use. Your letter to us was timely in that we have been discussing the possibility of discontinuing support. Are they aware of their responsibility to acknowledge those who have contributed to their support? Do they have a spirit of gratitude? Do they need counseling in this area? Is too much taken for granted?" *[Adapted from a letter received by this author.]*

A missionary friend wanted to get acquainted and to encourage the new pastor of a supporting church. She wrote a

"Such communication strengthens our own faith and let's us know that our support is needed."

personal note to him. No response. She wrote another. No response. Finally, after about five notes, written over several months, a letter came from the pastor.

At first he apologized for his long delay. Then, he explained. His explanation was something like this:

"I don't normally write. I usually have my secretary respond to letters. Even though your notes were encouraging it wasn't until you asked 'How can I pray for you and your family?' that I wanted to personally write to you."

Sincere, personal, encouraging notes *affect* the reader, generate response.

If you were to look at a large collection of missionary form letters, one of the things you would probably notice is the lack of personal notes.

If you asked your Christian friends questions like these: When you receive a printed letter from a missionary, what do you look for first? What causes you to read a missionary's newsletter? What do you think your friends would say?

When I've asked these kinds of questions in Sunday school classes and other gatherings, invariably the response is something like this:

"We look first to see if there is a personal note."

Many people not only look for the personal note, but base their decision to read the whole letter, or not, on whether there is a personal note.

The personal note not only *affects* the reader, but it may be the critical decision point as to whether a missionary newsletter is read at all.

Missionaries also say, when referring to their colleague's newsletters, "If there is a note, I'm more likely to read the letter."

To summarize what has been said so far about written communication, missionaries have to write to their partners, it's their lifeline. And, personalized correspondence is the best way to affect the reader.

Saying that may be a bit of a shock to some, since many missionaries rely upon the basic form letter as their mode of communication.

No doubt missionary form letters are important, but personalized correspondence is the strong link in the lifeline. The bond between a missionary and his friends is individualized, personalized communication.

Someone said, "It is not distance that separates us, but silence." It is certain that missionaries will be separated from their friends and family by great distances, and great spans of time. Distance and time plus silence are a deadly combination. It need not be deadly if silence is replaced by a consistent pattern of communication, with an emphasis upon personal correspondence.

"It is not distance that separates us, but silence."

Let's go back to the partnership model. It's important to realize partnership is always based upon personal relationships (trust) and service (value). Building and maintaining trust and demonstrating value are as much a part of written correspondence as they are a part of personal contact.

As we write, whether personal note or form letter, we need to keep in mind that our communication should enhance these pillars of partnership: trust and value.

Everyone likes to get personal notes and letters. There seems to be an upsurge of interest in the value of one-to-one communication through the personal note or letter. Probably this is due to the emphasis our culture has placed upon electronic communication: e-mail.

Missionaries are using e-mail more and more. In fact, electronic communication is becoming the medium of choice. There is nothing wrong with form letters, electronic messages, or even the telephone. But the personal, handwritten note has features no other form of communication possesses.

Remember Marshall McLuhen's statement: "The medium is the message." The medium through which a missionary communicates sends a message.

The medium is the message.

Pressing the point. Choosing the stationery, whether note or letter is a personal act. Personal style—some bit of the person, the writer—is conveyed through these choices.

Handwritten notes and letters carry a sense of personal knowledge and care for the reader. Effort is made with the reader in mind. Readers know this, perhaps by intuition, but they know they were thought of in a special way.

When doing workshops, I often ask in sessions about written communication, "When was the last time you wrote a personal note to one of your prayer or financial partners?"

Often the response to my question is "Does a telephone call count?"

What do you think? Should a telephone call count?

I know it's pretty "picky" to say, "No! Telephone calls don't count," but that's what I do say.

There is a reason. Telephone calls can't be kept. Telephone calls can't be pulled out of the drawer, trunk, or album days, weeks, or even years later—to once again be appreciated, savored, treasured.

Stoddard says, "A world of difference separates a phone call from a letter. The phone is a utility...A letter is a gift. Unlike the phone, a letter is never an interruption. A letter doesn't require immediate attention; it can be saved for the appropriate time and place and savored. Whenever I answer the telephone, I am at the mercy of another person's schedule. A letter, on the other hand, is a treat with no strings attached."[7]

Is this possible? A missionary's personal notes and letters as gifts? Yes, I think they are, or can be. And I think it's important for missionaries to realize how significant their personal notes and letters will be.

From this point on, in this chapter on the missionary's lifeline, the emphasis will be on writing personal notes. But it's also true that these principles are just as powerful in the longer letter.

When saying "personal note," I have a specific kind of note in mind. Notes are by nature short. I know a lot of missionaries will be glad to hear that! Norman Vincent Peale was said to be a prolific writer of inspirational notes. Peale's personal notes to friends and colleagues were usually not more than three sentences long.

According to note-writing etiquette, when using the one-fold type of note card commonly sold in stationery stores and in the note card sections of variety stores and grocery stores, the writer only has to write one page when the card is opened up, the facing page. Depending upon the size and style of the writer's handwriting, one to two short paragraphs fill this space.

Being a man, I especially appreciate this bit of etiquette. However, I've found that once I get started, it's amazing how much I think to say. (My wife is a natural communicator. She can write a significant note in the time it takes me to get the first three words down.)

In workshops, missionaries (yes, men too) are able to write a personal note, address the envelope, and put on the stamp in two minutes.

In two minutes you can *affect* someone's life.

In two minutes you can inspire, affirm, thank, encourage, and declare your affection and love for someone.

In two minutes you can minister.

"An inspired letter can be as riveting as a stare. It can move us to tears, spur us to action, provoke us, uplift us, touch us. Transform us."[8]

Writing these kinds of notes implies the missionary knows in some special and intimate ways the person or persons to whom he or she is writing.

In two minutes you can affect someone's life.

Going back to the idea of *personal relationships* in the model, do you see more fully what is meant by personal relationships? It's not merely being acquainted. It's knowing the person as much as is practical and possible. It means taking initiative to get to know the person. It means sharing lives—yours with theirs.

You cannot be a participant in another's life with strings attached. That is, as was said at the *value* point of the model, serve and minister with no strings attached. According to Stoddard, that's the beauty of a letter, there are no strings attached.

Therefore, write with no strings attached.

The intent of personal correspondence is to build up the other person—to encourage, to thank, to commend, to appreciate, to serve, to minister. These worthy goals will never be accomplished if there are strings attached; if we are attempting to get something out of it, even a written response.

You cannot participate in another's life if there are strings attached. Don't write to get; write to give.

Who should the missionary be writing to? At the least, he should write to everyone who made a commitment to pray and/or to give.

Husbands and fathers, lest you should think personal note writing is only for your wife, please give attention. If you don't already practice this kind of personal communication, assume it now as one of your responsibilities. You will make a difference in the lives of your partners.

Husbands and fathers, take this on with the assurance that you will be making a difference in the level of spiritual strength (prayer, encouragement and financial support) you and your family receive.

Besides thanking people for their partnership in giving and prayer, what else can be said? How do you commend, affirm, encourage, appreciate, love, etc?

Knowing the personal qualities of a friend or family member is a good beginning. In workshops the group collectively produces a list of all of the positive personality traits they can think of: goodness, loving, affectionate, truthful, encouraging, helpful, giving, listener, counselor, sense of humor, fun, available, trustworthy, etc. You could add to this list.

After coming up with a list of positive traits, each member of the group thinks of one person they would like to write a note to, right now, in two minutes!

Keillor suggests this: "Write the salutation—Dear You—and take a deep breath and plunge in. A simple declarative sentence will do, followed by another and another. As if you were talking to us. Don't think about grammar, don't think about style just give us your news. Where did you go, who did you see, what did they say, what do you think?"[9]

Keillor goes on to say, "If you don't know where to begin, start with the present: I'm sitting at the kitchen table on a rainy Saturday morning. Everyone is gone and the house is quiet. Let the letter drift along.... A letter is only a report to someone who already likes you ...."[10]

If you are reading this chapter and you are of the younger generation, can we [Stoddard, Keillor, and I] get you away from your computer long enough to write a handwritten note? You will if you think of your note as a gift.

If you are convinced of the importance of note writing, would you do something for me?

If you are convinced of the importance of personal note writing, would you do something for me? Find a piece of paper. It doesn't matter what it is. A page torn out of a magazine with some white space, a napkin, anything. If you have a note card or postcard at hand, use it. Now write a one- to two-paragraph note to someone you appreciate.

Tell them where you are, why you are writing right now, and anything else that pops into your mind, but tell them something that you appreciate about them.

Like this:

Dear Jim,

"I was just thinking about you. I didn't have anything to write on but this torn-out page. But I wanted you to know you are on my mind and I just thanked the Lord for how helpful you were at the end of the potluck last Friday. It didn't go unnoticed. You really lifted the load.

Thanks,
Jerry

Now, find an envelope—borrow, beg, steal—and get the address on it. Borrow a stamp if that's what it takes. Get it in the mail.

You've just done what this chapter has been all about.

Keep it up.

Get a supply of note cards, or postcards. Have your address list handy. Start writing notes that build bridges to people. Be vulnerable. Let your hair down. Be normal and natural. Say what's on your heart. Describe where you are right then, what you are doing, why, etc. Just get started.

Stoddard says, "Looking up at the clock on my desk, I once timed myself writing a brief note to a friend. It took me roughly four minutes, including addressing the envelope, putting on a stamp, even using sealing wax. My pocket calculator tells me that if I were to write three letters a day for one year, for a total of 1,095 letters, it would consume less than one percent of my time and cost less than one dinner for two out on the town.[11]

"If I were to write three letters [notes] a day for one year...it would consume less than one percent of my time."

Here's another example.

Dear Jim and Joyce,

I was just thinking about you, and shot up a word of prayer. How's little Billie doing? Betty and I have been thinking about him, about you, and praying. Keep us posted.

Love,
Barry and Betty

There it is. A two-minute note of concern, love, prayer, and friendship.

Yes, it could be an e-mail message, a telephone call, but remember, the medium is the message. The personal note card may be the most underused and undervalued medium in the domain of communications.

The medium is the message.

How often should missionaries write personal notes? To financial partners, once every two months. That's a suggestion.

A missionary could divide his list of financial partners into two groups. One month half of his partners receive a personal note; next month, the other half. These are notes in addition to the quarterly form letter. Yes, do write personal notes on form letters too. In fact, some missionaries leave a standing space in their form letters just for writing notes.

There's a potential problem with personal notes on form letters. If the missionary is using bulk mail rates, every letter must be identical. That eliminates personal notes.

This legal reality brings up a decision point. Should the missionary pay first-class rates in order to be able to write personal notes? Yes!

Some missionaries have mailing lists of hundreds of addresses. They should segment their mailing list and establish the group with which they have strong personal relationships (and/or with whom they will want to build relationships), but especially committed prayer and financial partners. These should get form letters as first-class mail, with personal notes. The others can be in the bulk-mail category.

Many missionaries have mailing services who put out their form letters. There is nothing wrong with this, but missionaries who use these services must realize what they are losing in the way of personal communication. They will need to find other ways to bridge the gap form letters alone will create.

Does e-mail bridge this gap? Yes, in many ways it can, but if you rely on e-mail, do all you can to personalize those electronic messages. Electronic messages do not, yet, substitute for the handwritten note. Perhaps there will come a day when technology will bridge that gap.

Hi Joe,

I wanted to let you know about the results of a note sent to my sister. I wrote to her during one of the times we had to write notes in the workshop. I was amazed at the results. This sister is also a sister in our Lord, but not a letter writer. She's always found the phone much handier to communicate with. Yes, with us being overseas, she doesn't phone because of the cost involved. But she doesn't write either, until…. That's right…after she received my note of thankfulness to God for her and the encouragement she has been, I received my first letter from her in seven years. [adapted from a real experience]

Not everyone will write back. One financial partner, when confronted by a missionary with the question, "Why don't you ever write?" responded, "I do write; I write every month."

This partner viewed his monthly check as personal correspondence. What missionary would argue?

In workshops, note writing may be done more than once over the course of several days. Often, before the workshop is over, one of the participants receives a warm answer from the person they wrote to.

One missionary received a response like this: "What an encouragement it was to get your note. You wouldn't believe what happened the day before your note came. Your note was so timely."

The writer of sincere personal notes *affects* the reader.

The personal note or letter is a basic tool of ministry. The form letter with a personal note can be.

Note writing is most effective, pleasurable, and easy if necessary tools are readily available.

A missionary I know has all the tools in a drawer right beside her favorite chair. In the evening while watching television she selects from her list of partners, or other friends, someone to whom she wants to write. She may be answering a note already received.

In the drawer are, besides the list of friends, a selection of note cards, postcards, stationery, colored pens (she varies the color mostly on the basis of the design of the note card she chooses for this particular note), address lists, and stamps. Being in the U.S., she is able to buy stamps with designs that appeal to her.

Note writing is easy if the right tools are handy.

She doesn't try to write a lot of notes in one evening. Her goal has been to write one note to one special person each evening. That's doable.

A missionary husband goes to a local McDonald's early on Saturday mornings with his address list, up-to-date financial records, selected note cards, and stamps. He stays there until his goal for the morning is reached. With this system he is able to write at least one personal note to each partner every two months.

Meanwhile, his wife is also involved in personal correspondence which sometimes overlaps his, and sometimes substitutes for his.

They found a good way to work as a team, but the husband bears a significant part of the load. In this way, both are building relationships with a number of people, including churches. Without making any overt efforts, and with no strings attached, they have seen a significant increase in partnership since, particularly, the husband got involved in writing personal notes.

Fountain pens are a particularly appropriate note-writing tool. In the U.S. culture it might seem as if the fountain pen is archaic, almost an artifact. However, not only has interest in writing personal letters grown but the manufacture of fine writing paper and fine writing instruments has also grown.

Some people believe fountain pens carry with them a certain aura, not a mystique, but a sense of class, distinction, and if you will, personality.

The power of the pen! "But what good is paper without a pen? Buying a fountain pen might have been one of the investments of my life. Writing is infinitely more satisfying when I use a fountain pen. The pen becomes a real extension of my arm, hand and heart. I get a thrill just hearing the squeak of my pen dashing acoss a blank page. When I'm thinking of what to say, I often hold my pen close to me and I can actually smell the ink, which has the scent of harsh soap. For me, the clicking of a computer or typewriter is just not the same."[12]

In the U.S. reliable fountain pens can be purchased for about $15.00.

Besides the fountain pen, or in lieu of the fountain pen, it is a good choice to invest in an inexpensive set of colored writing pens. These come with a variety of numbers of pens per set, with multiple colors. Writing with color provides an attractive, interesting dimension to the personal note.

Of course, the venerable ballpoint pen or pencil is a good writing instrument.

Stamp Art has become a popular method for the personally created, individualized, attractive, and interesting note card. With a blank piece of notecard-size card stock, ink pad, and stamp funny, colorful, seasonal, and topical cards are created.

Stamps with a wide variety of images are available. The rubber stamp comes affixed to a small block of wood. Color can be added to the stamp by using an ink pad, or by rubbing the stamp with a colored pen. Water soluble inks are used so that the stamp can be cleaned after use, and is then available for other projects.

Many print shops routinely throw away card stock of a size that could be easily adapted for creating note cards.

Software programs are available for most computers that

allow the user to create, design, and print personal note paper.

Missionaries overseas have resources that may not be readily available in the home country. Writing personal notes and letters on parchment, rice paper, paper available in the local market, banana leaves, bark, or other exotic items will usually attract attention and interest, especially if the item written upon can be directly related to an incident or to information mentioned in the note or letter.

Written communication is the missionary's lifeline, with the emphasis on life. Most missionaries, over the span of their careers, will see family, friends, and churches occasionally. The only consistent link to folks at home will be the written word.

In the judgment of this author, good writing is more important to the missionary than good speaking.

Good writing is more important than good speaking.

So, missionary, where are you putting your strokes?

Even with all that has been said in this chapter, missionary newsletters will continue to be the backbone of missionary communication. However, if newsletters are going to be read by anyone but the missionary's mother, newsletters will have to be done well.

In the next chapter you will find some tips on how to make an attractive, readable, illuminating, exciting, and inspirational newsletter.

But don't forget that personal note.

END NOTES

[1] Garrison Keillor, *How to Write a Personal Letter*, 1967, Condensed from an advertisement, International Paper Co., New York, N.Y.

[2] Keillor, *How to Write a Personal Letter*, p. 130.

[3] Alexandra Stoddard, *Gift of a Letter*, 1990, Doubleday, New York, N.Y., p. 4. Stoddard's small book is the most inspiring and helpful book on the art of writing notes and letters that has come to the attention of this author. This book should be in every missionary's collection of materials for writing, right along with pens, stamps, and stationery.

[4] Stoddard, *Gift of a Letter*, p. 9.

[5] Keillor, *How to Write a Personal Letter*, p. 131.

[6] Harvey S. Wiener, *Any Child Can Write*, 1990, Rev. Ed., Bantam Books, New York, N.Y., p. 58.

[7] Stoddard, *Gift of a Letter*, p. 10.

[8] Stoddard, *Gift of a Letter*, p. 4.

[9] Keillor, *How to Write a Personal Letter*, p. 131.

[10] Keillor, *How to Write a Personal Letter*, p. 131.

[11] Stoddard, *The Gift of a Letter*, p. 66.

[12] Stoddard, *The Gift of a Letter*, p. 100.

CHAPTER TEN
• • • • • • • • •

Creating An Attractive Newsletter

The most important contact piece you will have with your partners is your frequent newsletter. This will keep them up on the progress of your work and news of your family. But if it comes in an unattractive format, or is difficult to read, your partners will probably lay it aside for more pressing things.

If you already have a computer for your work, I would highly recommend you get a good page-layout program and learn to use it to produce your newsletters. If you do not have access to a good computer system, get in touch with someone who can help you and get them to read this chapter. With the computer all things are possible at your fingertips to produce a really attractive letter—one that will impress your readers and get your message across.

Knowing how to use the computer to achieve this is what this chapter is all about. For hundreds of years the secrets of graphic design were known only to trained designers or typesetters. Now it is at your command, too, but few people know the secrets of good design and typesetting. I have tried to boil centuries of design secrets down to these few. Keep your eyes open for good ideas and adapt them to your publications.

WRITING A GOOD LETTER

A well-written letter to your partners is worth its weight in gold! Some people are naturally fair to good writers, others really struggle to put thoughts on paper. But everyone needs help with producing an interesting and attractive publication that will link them to supporters and friends.

Before you even start to write, get organized! It is hard to sit down to write a letter without any thought-through items. Keeping a journal or diary helps, but a wall calendar with big squares is a perfect place to jot down things that might be something for the newsletter. Note events in your work and also in the family. When it comes time to write, you will have an excess of material to include. Cull out the most interesting and meaningful and use them. Also, if possible, use a camera to record events. A digital camera is a real asset for this. Having photos on hand, instead of at the developers, means you will be more likely to include them. A picture is worth a thousand words and thought-provoking captions will be even more valuable.

If you have children, their comments and observations, drawings, stories, etc. will add interest to your communication. They are your partners too.

Try not to write about the same things every letter. Vary letters with background material of your ministry; the ideas and cultural concepts of those you minister to are very important. Reactions and quotes from them can be very interesting.

Be honest about your ministry. The ups and the downs should be included, but never with a negative tone. Showing the downs gives your partnership something to pray about.

Now comes the hardest part—editing your writing. Go through it to eliminate excess words and unclear writing. Have a second person read and make suggestions. Watch for and remove repetitious wording and ideas.

Check your spelling and the *proper* use of words.

ORGANIZE YOUR INFORMATION

A well-organized newsletter is a joy to read. People appreciate conciseness and organization and it gives a good impression of your thinking processes.

First of all, group similar information together (addresses, etc.), Use a box or panel area to set apart information or gather small bits of info into a larger unit. Group photos into a design element rather than scatter photos through the text (it makes it look spotty). Make little sketches of possible arrangements of the material in your newsletter before you ever sit down to the computer.

"What more can I do to make my letter hang together?"

There are some editorial devices and some graphic devices that may help in your information organization.

Editorially, you may try to use *alliteration,* starting each section or piece of information with the same letter of the alphabet. Enlarge that letter or set it in a different typeface to emphasize it.

Write your letter around a *theme* and use appropriate display type to illustrate the theme. Use art appropriate to the theme.

Repetition is another useful organizer. Using the same phrase or thought throughout the letter helps hang it together.

Graphic devices are many, but do not try to use them all in the same letter.

Repetition is probably the most used. Using the same shape of picture or panel or boxes is often used. Repeating type faces or sizes is effective also. But using too many boxes or panels can make the letter appear cluttered.

Alternation is important visually. It gives a lot of interest to the layout and breaks up the static feel. The page to the right uses both alternation and repetition.

Gradation is using either type and/or graphic elements in graduated sizes to give variety or importance to various parts of

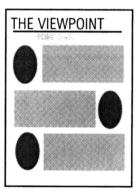

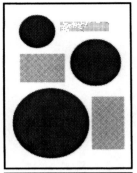

Cats—
Pets or Pests
Cat Myths

Cat

Carl's Currents
Coastal Victory

Midnight Adventure

Circle of Support

the letter. Set the most important information in larger type, that's what your reader will see first.

Sometimes gradation is important in establishing dominance in a page design. Larger things are naturally more dominant. All good designs have something that is more dominant and then there is a string of dominance leading the reader through the material in a natural way. In the design to the left the reader is led from the top left (natural place to begin reading) by a graduating dominant string to the most dominant element at the bottom, a sort of climax to your message.

Use graduated type sizes to help the reader follow the text. We are so familiar with this device that we unconsciously follow the direction the designer wants us to read by starting with the larger title type and working down through subtitles, etc. (Titles should be larger than subtitles, etc.) Lead-in copy (decks—discussed later) should be a little larger than the text type. Be consistent in the sizes of type you choose for dominance.

Direction is another very subtle device you may use to help your reader through the copy. Notice the use of the cats in the second picture—they point the reader into the next text. If you wish the reader to read across the page, use horizontal lines, if you wish them to read vertically, use vertical rules to force the direction up and down.

Another way to organize information is to use *boxes* or *panels* to separate out important or supplementary information like addresses, announcements, etc. There will be ideas for boxes and panels a little later in this chapter, but it is important to think about their use as your letter begins to take form.

Don't forget to think in terms of charts, graphs, maps, calendars and other visual ways of presenting a lot of complicated material in interesting picture forms. Graphs and charts are great for showing comparisons and progress of support raising, progress in work and many other aspects of your work and life.

CHOOSE GOOD READABLE TYPE

Type is the tone of voice you are using in your letter. The choice of type may make a letter more formal, casual, or downright yucky.

There are literally hundreds of typefaces available to the computer user. The more decorative the type, the more distracting it is to read. The most common type in use is the Times family. It is a plain type, very readable, and combines well with other type styles. It is a serif type, the little hooks on the letters help the eye track along the line. This book is set with Adobe Caslon, another attractive and easy to read serif type. Serif type is best used for the blocks of text in your letter since it is easier to read.

Sans serif type is without the little hooks and is a little more difficult to read in blocks of text. Sans serif type needs to have more white space around it to be readable. It is a good type to make bold for titles, subtitles and photo captions, and in contrast to the serif text type. Helvetica, Optima, Officina sans, are all good typefaces.

Script typefaces are the third kind. Script is hard to read in big blocks of text but may be used for invitations, poetry, announcements and tidbits of information. Script comes in all styles, from formal to handwritten copy. Never use all caps with script typefaces, it is very difficult to read.

The fourth category of typefaces are all the fancy types called display types. These may be chosen to support the theme of the publication or as a decorative punch, but never use them for blocks of text. A little goes a long way.

A little-known family of typefaces are the dingbats, little pieces of art that may be used to decorate your publication, or for emphasis of points in text. The most common are the Zaph Dingbats but there are several others available for the computer. Made large, they can be attractive pieces of art.

Typefaces have within them families of fonts. Fonts are the

Serif type
Times Roman
New Century Schoolbook
Palatino
Melior

Sans serif type
Helvetica
Optima
Officina Sans
Helvetica
Optima
Officina Sans

Script type
Commercial
Cascade
Nuptial
Brush Hand
Calligraphic

Display type
Bordeaux
Beguiat
Improv
SHOT THRU

Dingbats
✳☐✲▼✳✳▲◎○

Times normal
Times bold
Times italic
Times bold italic

Times
Helvetica
Perlapt

Type sizes
Times 9 points
Times 10 points
Times 11 points
Times 12 points
Times 13 points
Times 18 pts

Times 10 point text with no leading between the lines.

Times 10 point text with 20% leading—2 extra points between the lines.

Times 10 point text with 40% leading (14 pts) between the lines.

styles within typefaces such as bold, italic, condensed, expanded, etc. A good-looking letter can be done using just one typeface but using bold, italic and bold italic, as well as varying the sizes of type within the typeface.

When considering combining typefaces, use the *rule of three:* one serif type, one sans serif type and either one script or one display type for emphasis. (Dingbats don't count in this rule.) Make sure there is enough contrast one from the other and they look good together. Avoid extremes in typestyles, and keep appropriateness to the message in mind.

Type comes in different sizes and on the computer it is possible to define the size down to hundredths of an inch. The most comfortable sizes for text is usually between 10 and 12 points for books. The choice depends on the reader's preferences and the length of line. The longer the line the larger the text should be. The norm is 45 to 54 characters for medium size type. (The width of the text in this book is the optimum line length for this size type.) It is very difficult to read long lines of very small type.

Another consideration in typesetting is the amount of space between lines. This is called leading (leding). The term comes from the old hot type system of typesetting where thin strips of lead were placed between the lines of letters to space out the text. *It is the space and not the type size that makes text readable.* For the best readability there should be about 20 percent extra space between lines and on the computer this is usually the amount in *auto*, although this percentage may be changed in the preferences. Keep the leading in all your text uniform; don't add or subtract it to make the text fit into your space. It is better to cut a few words or reword something to make the text fit.

Be consistent in the type sizes you use for subtitles, etc. By using style sheets in setting up letters and other publications, controlling the consistency of type sizes and styles is a lot easier.

USE COLUMNS

Type is kept in order in a layout by placing it in columns. The graphic designer uses columns to give order and alignment to the page. Underlying a good page layout is a grid. On the computer a simple grid is made when margins and space between columns are decided. The actual grid is never seen but is essential to give the page a foundation. Many designers also divide the page into quarters or eights horizontally to help with placement of photos, titles, etc.

There are several choices to make in choosing the number and widths of columns on the page. One may choose to have a single column of type on the page or several, depending on the desired look of the piece.

A single column of type is used for letters, books, etc. Margins should be wide and type should be larger. Extra leading space will help the reader cope with long lines of type.

Two even columns on a page is often used for newsletters. Narrower outside margins may be used and the division between columns (gutter) should be between one and two picas (.165 to .33 of an inch) in width. Another way of doing two columns is to have a narrow and a wide column. This will allow a little more visual interest on the page. Smaller type can be used in narrower columns. If the publication is two-sided, use the same columns on the back.

Some people like three columns on an 8.5-inch page. The outside margins may be narrower but not less than a half inch. The gutters should not be wider than 2 picas or .33 of an inch. This style is called a newspaper layout. It allows for stretching photos across two of the columns or narrow photos within a column. If the article is long, titles may be stretched across two or three columns or confined to a single column. This adds great visual interest.

A magazine format allows for more flexible columns to fit

This is justified type, both margins are even and easy to read. Justifying type without hyphenations may create big gaps in these columns. Use the hyphenation mode to avoid the problem.

Flush left typesetting is easier to read but avoid big variations in line lengths—it gives the page a ragged look.

A flush right column is not so easy to read in big clumps of type.

Centered type may be used for short photo captions, poetry, etc. —never for large amounts of text.

around photos, art and captions. It is basically a one-column grid but the type in the column varies in width and allows more flexibility in using pictures, etc.

In typesetting, four basic type column styles are commonly used. The most familiar columns are the flush left column, either justified to give an even right edge or left unjustified to make a ragged right edge. A justified column means there will be uneven letter and word spacing in the lines as the computer tries to fit as much on a line as is technically possible. The ragged right format means the word and letter spacing will be even. This is less distracting to the reader but gives a more informal look to the publication.

A flush right column has a ragged left margin and a straight right margin. Readers are used to starting each line at the same margin so ragged right in a large text block is uncomfortable to read. Word breaks are also a problem so it is best to turn off hyphenation to prevent funny-looking word breaks. If the right margin turns out too ragged looking, use discretionary hyphenation. Use ragged right columns for photo captions and sometimes poetry or ad copy.

Centered columns should be used only for poetry or announcements. They are extremely uncomfortable to read in large blocks of copy. Centered type is the easiest to use for titles, subtitles, etc. as in this book.

There are some important rules to keep in mind for columns.

Use a type size appropriate to the width of the column as mentioned in the type section. Don't use large type in a narrow column. If the size of type makes you uncomfortable it is probably the wrong size. Experiment until it feels right.

If you are justifying type, watch for stacking hyphens at the end of the lines. Avoid using more than three hyphens in a stack.

Justified type sometimes leaves holes or rivers of white space between words. Not using hyphenation or using too narrow a column causes this. Use discretionary hyphenation to close up the holes.

The standard of good typesetting is to never put more than **one** space between words or sentences. This is the one big difference between the typewriter and typesetting copy.

VARY FOLDS AND FORMATS

Another important thing to consider, right along with columns as you plan your letter, is what format to use and how to fold the letter for mailing. Many times the folding helps determine the format and columns of a letter. They create "pages."

There are several types of letter formats. The most common is the classic letter (8.5 x 11 inches) or legal size (8.5 x 14 inches) with one- or two-sided printing. This may be a single column, uneven columns or divided into two or three columns of type.

But the 8.5 x 11-inch or 14-inch (legal) letter may be folded in half to make a booklet style. The inside of the booklet style gives a bigger area for photo layouts. For the smaller booklet, a one-column format works best, the legal-size booklet may use two columns. Use a half-inch margin for booklet styles.

Brochure folds give even more variety to the look of a letter. Doing the brochure style allows for a more flexible layout. The 11-inch page may be folded in thirds and the legal size into four sections. Each section should contain a single column of type. The margins may be a minimum of two picas (.33 inch) and the gutters twice the width of the margin so when the letter is folded the type is centered in the columns. Reserving the back for addresses and taping the edges shut, you may send it without an envelope (a self-mailer).

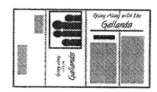

Two things you should avoid with folds. *Never* place blocks of text type across a vertical fold. This is very distracting to the reader. Titles and captions may be placed across a fold but be careful about the fold going through characters or words. Also avoid folding across faces in photos.

NAMEPLATES

After deciding the basic format, type and column layout of the newsletter, it is time to add the visually interesting features that give the sparkle to a publication.

The nameplate at the top of the letters is a good place to start. It is the title of the publication and sets the tone of the publication as well as identifies the sender.

The nameplate is not the place for addresses, phone numbers, etc. This information should be placed elsewhere. Choose a title that reflects the family or yourself, and the work you are doing. It may be used to identify location in general. A letter from a family usually has the last name in the title; for a single person, the first name may be used. Avoid, if possible, words like Bulletin, News, Letter. Sometimes a title with alliteration is attractive (*Rinker's Review, Shirley Shares*). *From the Sahara Sands, Fred's Flight Log, Wright's Data, Davis.com,* all reflect location and/or work. The typeface for the nameplate should reinforce the title. Find a typeface that illustrates the title.

In the nameplate also include the issue number information and the date. It is best to give a general date, May 2006, rather than a specific date, in case the letters don't get sent when planned. Some people use seasons (Spring 2006) rather than months.

Make the nameplate a strong element in the newsletter. Use strong large type and artwork that is suitable. Some like to include a recent family photo in the nameplate area—good idea! This helps readers recognize family members. Use a variety of type sizes and make sure there are no conflicts between the various elements of the nameplate.

Avoid placing the nameplate in a box. Using a box draws

attention away from the typed message. Use bars and lines for separation if needed, and vary type sizes to give visual variety to the nameplate.

BOXES AND PANELS

Boxes and panels are very useful in a newsletter but should be used carefully and with purpose. There is a tendency to overuse them. One or two on a page should be the limit.

Boxes and panels can be used not only to group items together, but also to separate supplementary information from the basic letter and make it important.

A box is an area usually bounded on all four sides by lines. The inside may be white, black or colored with shades of color or grey. A panel, to be technical, doesn't have bounding lines. It is usually black, grey or colored.

Boxes and panels do not have to be plain. They can be added to or subtracted from by other shapes. They can be made into free-form shapes or rotated to add wonderful visual interest. Type may be placed in them. Just make sure the type has good contrast with the background and is big enough to be seen well.

Another important rule for type inside a box or panel is to keep at least 1 pica (.165 of an inch) of space between the boundary of box or panel and the type within. Placing type too close to the edge gives a crowded feeling.

Don't use small type over a grey background unless you are using a 600 dpi printer. Very course gray screens conflict with the type. Also, never place type over a background that conflicts with it.

Also be careful with contrast between type and the background. Using white type (reversed type) over a light grey background doesn't give good contrast.

Be careful when reversing white letters out of a dark background. Using serif type with its thick and thin lines may mean

A box or panel can be used to set off important news or announcement, an interesting happening, quip, comment or quote. It can also contain addresses, etc.

It can be a different typeface or font of the typeface used in the letter and may be a different size.

REMEMBER THE MEETING JANUARY 25, AT 6 P.M. AT TRINITY CHURCH

Don't get too close to the edges of the box or panel. Be careful to have good contrast between type and background. **Use bold type to improve contrast.** Don't use serif type if the narrow lines disappear. **Use bold for better contrast.**

Too many boxes make a broken-up page.

	hairline
	1 point
	2 point
	3 point
	8 point
	12 point

Bar with dingbat art in it.

This is a sample of ragged right type with a very thin rule to separate it from the ragged right column of text next to it. It gives the eye a stopping place.	This is a sample of ragged right type with a very thin rule to separate it from the ragged right column of text next to it.

that some of the letters will look broken up. If you must use it, make the type bold. Sans serif type works better, especially in the smaller type sizes.

Don't overdo boxes on a letter. One or two on a side is adequate. Also try to use the same type of box or panel to give the publication a unified look.

Be careful with boxes when you are also using lines (rules) or bars on the same page. They can become really distracting if they do not work together. The best rule is *less is better.*

BARS AND RULES

Sometimes a simple line or two added to the newsletter really dresses it up. It is amazing how lines and bars seem to anchor the letter and emphasize sections.

Lines are usually any width up to 12 points. Bars are usually thicker. Lines and bars do not have to be plain. Making them out of dingbats or adding dingbat shapes to them really can create an original look.

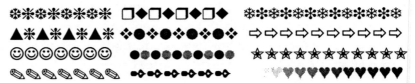

Combining type with lines or bars also adds to the visual attraction. • • • • • • • • • **More in a minute!**

Rules can be used to enclose copy or create a border. If copy is already justified you don't need a line between columns. If the edge is ragged right, sometimes a line seems to even up and separate the columns.

Wisely used lines add balance to a layout, visual interest, unite similar items and separate item or columns from the main text. They say real graphic thought went into the letter design. Don't use too many on a page nor different styles of lines.

PHOTOS

A picture is worth a thousand words. This is true not only for transmitting information but for adding visual interest to a layout. The hardest job is getting good pictures that tell a story.

Keep your camera handy and use it often. Record your life and family activities, as well as your ministry opportunities. A good digital camera and a computer are a great combination—no time lost waiting for film development. Read up on the techniques of photography. A good photo is invaluable.

Each photo used should have a message and add to your communication. It should be clear and have good contrast. Faces should not be heavily shadowed or too dark. If you scan a colored photograph to make a black and white photo, make sure the faces are not too red, they will turn out very dark. This can be corrected using a program like Photoshop.

It is easy to edit, enlarge or reduce, crop and place photos with a computer. Crop means eliminating excess parts of a photo to emphasize the subjects. Prevent a tight crowded feeling by leaving a little background around the subject, especially above the head. When cropping, be careful not to crop off tops of heads, fingers, feet, etc. Bodies are most comfortably cropped at the waist or mid-chest or at the knees if it is impossible to include the whole body.

Photographs may be improved using the adjustment tools in a photo correction program—crop tool, auto-contrast, curves, brightness/contrast and the burn and dodge tools.

Some pictures cannot be salvaged. They may look great in color but in black and white everything is lost.

Cropping and using the curve tool brings the subject to the foreground.

Never place a picture with the subject or object facing off the page. Move the photo to other side of page. Don't flop it!

A light border line frames and encloses the photo, and completes the photo where there is a light area at the edge.

Scattered pictures give a choppy appearance.

When using a group of photos in your publication, try grouping them together with captions. Groupings are dramatic. Try to make the photos similar in size, either by height or width, to avoid a ragged look. Use them in a series to tell a story, show a process or the progression of an event. Take a look at the various layouts of pages illustrated in this chapter to see how groupings strengthen a layout.

WAKE UP YOUR PUBLICATION

Look at your "plain Jane" letter and think about giving it a bit of graphic punch. If you can't think of ways to improve its graphic appeal, draw others into the process of brainstorming the graphics. Look for ideas from other letters and publications to give you ideas.

Ask yourself:

• What other type do I have that will convey the theme or focus better?
We may be tempted to use fancy types for our block of text—this is tiring to read.

• What type can I use for titles, subtitles, etc., that will perk up the message and layout?

• Have I written the text with readers in mind, making it as interesting as possible? Sometimes adding a little background information makes the article much more interesting.

• Have I created an appealing nameplate for my publication? This can be made into a family project.

• Have I done a thorough editing and spell check on this letter? Don't trust your computer spell check, it doesn't know or catch everything! Have I had at least two other people read this publication?

• Have I checked this for consistency? See the next two pages for things to check.

NEWS FROM THE HARTS IN GHANA
JULY 2006

The Effects of Worship in Our Church

Studying the recent growth in the local churches in Tamale, Ghana, we have discovered that one of the most powerful tools of evangelism is Christ-centered worship in music and praise. The curious come to see and hear how Christians truly worship in the church and stay to hear the Good News of salvation through Jesus.

The church leadership has been encouraging worship leaders to write their own praises to the Lord and to incorporate testimonies and devotional thoughts that develop the theme of the worship service. They are also encouraging non-leaders to participate in the services along with the worship leladers.

And the church has doubled its attendance in a year.

Building Worship

How is all this happening? Building concepts of worship and all the ideas that can be used has been the focus with worship leaders for the last 18 months. There has been in-depth study of true scriptural worship in small groups.

But beyond the concepts, the leaders and others have been practicing worship together in small groups and they have been very enthusiastic about the changes true worship are bringing to their own lives. They are beginning to live lives of praise and thankfulness.

Worship has also been spreading through their families. When the families come together in the church, they are already primed to worship and not afraid to express worship openly in the services.

Blessing through Worship

Because neighbors and friends have been attracted by the attitude of worship in our local church members, there have been many opportunities to share with them the story of God's redeeming love. There is nothing mrore attractive than a joyous heart in the face of need and difficulties and sadness. Praise and worship express trust in the promises of God, and the power He has to act in our everyday lives. A praising church is a powerful witness!

Addresses:
Field   **Home**

Heartbeats from Ghana

Events in the lives of the Bill Harts and the church in Ghana

July 2006   **21st Message**

Discovering the Power of Worship in Evangelism

Studying the recent growth in the local churches in Tamale, Ghana, we have discovered that one of the most powerful tools of evangelism is Christ-centered worship in music and praise. The curious come to see and hear how Christians truly worship in the church and stay to hear the Good News of salvation tthrough Jesus.

The church leadership has been encouraging worship leaders to write their own praises to the Lord and to incorporate testmonies and devotional thoughts that develop the theme of the worship service. They are also encouraging non-leaders to participate in the services along with the worship leaders.

And the church has doubled its attendance in a year.

Building Worship

How is all this happening? Building concepts of worship and all the ideas that can be used has been the focus with worship leaders for the last 18 months. There has been in-depth study of true scriptural worship in small groups.

But beyond the concepts, the leaders and others have been practicing worship together in small groups and they have been very enthusiastic about the changes true worship are bringing to their own lives. They are beginning to live lives of praise and thankfulness.

Worship has also been spreading through their families. When the families come together in the church, they are already primed to worship and not afraid to express worship openly in the services.

Blessing through Worship

Because neighbors and friends have been attracted by the attitude of worship in our local church members, there have been many opportunities to share with them the story of God's redeeming love. There is nothing more attractive than a joyous heart in the face of need and difficulties and sadness. Praise and worship express trust in the promises of God, and the power He has to act in our everyday lives. A praising church is a powerful witness!

Addresses:
Field   Home

- Is the type attractive and readable, a good size for your readers?
- Do the typefaces work well together? Is there good contrast?
- Do they support the focus/theme of the publication?
- Will this type give good results on the printer?
- Is the spacing consisent between lines, sections and paragraphs?
- Are the margins even and the columns aligned top and bottom?
- Does the page have unity? Balance? Contrast?
- Have I used appropriate artwork, panels, bars, lines,etc.? Have I used too many?
- Are the pages balanced and related to each other?
- Are the photos, artwork and/or illustrations clear, appropriate and aid the story?
- Are the photos, maps and other illustrations placed attractively in the layout and large enough to be useful?
- Have I included all the addresses and other essential information needed by the reader?
- Have I checked every-thing for **consistency** of fonts, typefaces and size, as well as line spacing?

good photo spacing

bad photo spacing

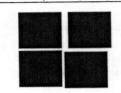

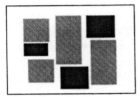

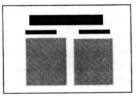

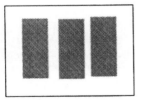

CHECKING YOUR WORK IS *ABSOLUTELY* ESSENTIAL

You may feel you are finished with your publication but one more step is essential—evaluating and checking the page(s).

Consistency is the one thing that makes a good publication.

Ask yourself these questions about your publication:

- Is there consistent space above and below titles, subtitles, etc., and consistent spacing between photos, and between photos and the captions? Keeping the spacing even really gives unity to the design.
- Are the margins, gutters and top and bottom borders equal?
- Are the typefaces, styles and sizes of titles, subtitles, etc., consistent with each other? Are they all italicized? Bold?
- Have I been consistent in the use of lines, bars, etc.? Are they all equal in size, length, shading, etc.
- Check alignment of numbers, periods, decimals, etc., in text and indexes as well as in charts, lists, graphs.
- If you have used centered titles, etc, are they all centered or are some a bit off center? Sometimes the indenting for the text can cause problems with centering.
- Check for consistent spelling of foreign words. Provide a pronunciation clue to help your reader.
- Check for alignment of paragraphs in a column. If the column is made up of different blocks of type, it is easy to get them misaligned.
- Check the tops and bottoms of columns of type—they should align exactly, unless you purposely opt for irregular columns.

Now put your publication aside and come back to it tomorrow or at another time and look at it critically again. You will be surprised at what you see with fresh eyes.

Following these suggestions you will develop your skills as a graphic publisher. The principles in this chapter can be applied to all printed materials you do, plus your Web sites.

A Bit More History

At the close of the Preface to this book I encouraged the reader to read the book actively and to listen for the ring of truth.

Of course, I won't know how most purchasers respond to the principles, use the ideas, or evaluate the usefulness of the material.

Over the years, though, I have received a considerable amount of feedback as this material was presented in a variety of settings and situations: one-to-one consulting and workshops; over the telephone, and via e-mail or fax; in cross-cultural settings involving as many as nine different cultures in one workshop; on napkins in restaurants; and, over time, with several hundred missionaries from several mission agencies.

There are at least three mission agencies who have adopted these materials—particularly the biblical teaching and the partnership model as the basis for training their own missionaries to do partnership development.

You know, Jesus said it was not a good idea to *build a house on sand.* As you also know from the chapter "One Man's Story," I did just that. As I studied the Scriptures and the history of "live-by-faith-alone," I realized Scripture was solid rock. I realized, too, the ideology of living-by-faith-alone was sand. The word "alone" is an important clarifying word.

For your encouragement, I want to quote a few people who have sent me notes expressing their gratitude for helping them to better understand what raising support is all about, and for helping them make progress in this challenging endeavor; helping them, if you will, build their support raising structure on rock. I have not altered these notes except for what's in backets.

Our appreciation of thanks can't express our appreciation of both of you [including Dona]. All have expressed how much they've learned from the workshop—above the concept [of raising support] is the examples of your lives. Thank you for being so humble and transparent with us.

I just wanted to say thank you for all of the help you have been to me. Your wisdom and insightful presentations have helped me during this last month.

Thanks!! I really appreciated your sincerity, your insight and your foundational emphasis on the Word. Thanks for all the help you've been to me.

Thanks for being so real. Thanks too for all the useful stuff.

Thanks for your undistorted view of partnership.

Thanks so much for your wise counsel concerning finances. I called [their organization], started to check into other churches for support, extended our mailing list, ordered response envelopes, and better organized our budget. Your advice was greatly appreciated by my wife and I, and our church. We thought it was great how even though you are not in [their organization] you were so willing to help. We hope and pray that God continues to bless you and your ministry.

I just want to say how your life is continuing to bless people. Chris and I have now taught 96 [members of their organization] and all feel very positive about it. We also have helped several individuals who could not for some reason or other make it to the work-

shops. So, this Christmas, your gift of this course keeps giving and giving and I just want to say thank you.

I just wanted to jot you a note of thanks for the many valuable insights and truths you have shared these few days. The openness with which you have shared from your own experience has really touched me. I arrived for this furlough in a very drained condition, and not sure I could face visiting with my constituency. Several months of rest have helped a lot, but this workshop has come at the perfect time to get my thinking straightened out and provide me with excellent ideas to use with my partners. Thank you so much for coming.

You can tell there has been much encouragement over the years. I've shared just some of the notes. I trust you will understand quoting these missionaries is not meant as a venture into an ego trip. I want you to know that raising support is a challenge for most of us, and the ideas in this book have helped a lot of people meet that challenge.

Let me relate one other personal situation. I'm now sixty-eight years old. Early this year one of our supporting churches had to cut back on giving to their missionaries. Our support from this church was cut almost in half: by $250 per month.

I told the missions pastor that it was really going to be hard, maybe even at my age impossible, to generate $250 of new support. I have to admit to you that this situation hit me pretty hard. I admit I was, before the Lord, a little grumpy about it.

But we went to God and began praying for some new partners. We told our friends through our newsletter what had happened and that we needed to make up that loss. Some of them began to pray. We mentioned the need in three successive newsletters, and reported on what was happening.

In about six months, as a result, I believe, of the fact that we had never stopped doing what I've been writing about in this book, the gap was closed.

I need to say, too, that along with our "doing," we could see how the Lord superintended the process that produced that result. We have one new church, and five new couples who, together, closed the gap. Even at our ages raising support is possible, which I wasn't sure about.

God's people are concerned about missions and about missionaries. This has been proven over and over again in our own lives, and in the lives of countless missionaries.

As I bring closure to this book, I want to draw your attention to two verses of Scripture. The Holy Spirit used these verses to get me headed in the right direction in the challenge of partnership development.

"The workman deserves his wages" (Luke 10:7, Phillips).

"All scripture is inspired by God and is useful for teaching the faith and correcting error, for resetting the direction of a man's life and training him in good living. The scriptures are the comprehensive equipment of the man of God, and fit him fully for all branches of his work" (2 Timothy 3:16, Phillips).

In the first ten years of our lives as faith missionaries I had never once considered that I was a workman who deserved my wage. I never once thought this statement applied to faith missionaries. The realization that this was an error in my thinking changed my belief system. When I realized that God meant for missionaries to have their wage, well, that changed everything.

That statement—*the workman deserves his wages*—is not a promise, but a governing principle. It became the cornerstone of my restructured thinking.

It's said many times in many ways throughout the Bible, *"Thy word is truth."*

May this book have the ring of truth.

Sincerely,
Paul I. Johnson

Printed in the United States
76232LV00004B/20